MORE LIVES THAN ONE?

'With a free and open mind I listen attentively to the Indian doctrine of rebirth and look around in the world of my own experience to see whether somewhere and somehow there is some authentic sign pointing towards reincarnation.'

C. G. JUNG

MORE LIVES THAN ONE?

The Evidence of the Remarkable Bloxham Tapes

JEFFREY IVERSON

Foreword by Magnus Magnusson

SOUVENIR PRESS

First published 1976 by Souvenir Press Ltd,
43 Great Russell Street, London WC1B 3PA
and simultaneously in Canada by
Methuen Publications,
Agincourt, Ontario

ISBN 0 285 62239 0

Printed in Great Britain by
Clarke, Doble & Brendon Ltd,
Plymouth

CONTENTS

FOREWORD

IN my years as a journalist and broadcaster, I have explored
some very odd stories indeed. Many of them have been real-
life detective stories from the past, like the story of the princess in China who committed suicide after being falsely
accused of treason, or the story of the heretic Pharaoh who
married the most beautiful woman in the world (Nefertete) and
was expunged from the official pages of history. Some have
been forgeries or frauds, like the great Piltdown Man hoax.
Some have been the result of self-delusion, like the woman in
Scotland who claimed to be Christ reincarnated and founded
a sect known as the Nameless Ones.

But the story told in this book must rank as the most intriguing story I've ever covered – because it contains all the
elements of oddness and detective work and sheer *strangeness*
that add up to a great mystery.

It all started right out of the blue, as far as I was concerned.
A BBC television producer in Cardiff, Jeff Iverson (the author
of this book), telephoned me one day to ask if I would like to
do a programme on hypnosis. But not just *any* programme on
hypnosis – a rather special one. Because, as he explained, there
was a distinguished hypnotherapist in Cardiff, a Mr Arnall
Bloxham, who claimed that scores of his patients under hypnosis remembered and experienced a previous life, a previous
incarnation on earth – and sometimes several. Since I was
interested in history and archaeology, would I like to under-
take a cool, impartial, informed and critical look at these
claims? Were they genuine cases of 'regression' into other
lives?

I didn't hesitate for a moment. Like everybody else, I knew

of the strange case of 'Bridey Murphy' – the young American housewife who, during repeated sessions under hypnosis, had experienced in vivid and accurate detail the life of a young Irish girl of that name in the nineteenth century. I knew vaguely of several other bizarre cases, all apparently inexplicable, of people under hypnosis speaking in languages they had never learned, or showing intimate knowledge of countries they had never visited and historical periods they had scarcely even heard of.

So I went to Cardiff to start my investigation into these claims. What it became, in fact, was an investigation into the human mind itself. It was an uncanny experience to listen to a woman who had never been to York reliving, in remarkable detail and unfeigned terror, the experiences of a young Jewess in York during the great Jewish Massacre; or a man who had never been to sea in his life (or in *this* life, one should perhaps say) experiencing a sea battle in a British frigate blockading the French coast during the Napoleonic wars, and having his leg shot off. Jeff Iverson and I followed the trail as far as we could. We visited places where these 'regressions' were set. We checked and cross-checked against known or presumed historical facts. We spoke to historians, archaeologists, archivists, psychologists. We dug and we delved, we questioned and we argued.

Were the details accurate? Where and how could these people have acquired the period detail that came welling up out of their minds under hypnosis? Could it be a deliberate hoax? And if not – was there a rational explanation for this phenomenon? Racial memory? Dreaming? Or hidden memories coming to the surface of the mind from deep in the subconscious?

And the result of this journey of investigation? That must be up to the individual readers of this book to decide. But to me at least there is one incontrovertible conclusion – that the human mind is an infinitely more complex, mysterious and fascinating thing than we can even imagine.

MAGNUS MAGNUSSON

ACKNOWLEDGEMENTS

The author wishes to thank the British Broadcasting Corporation for giving him permission to write this book, and to quote material from a documentary film, 'The Bloxham Tapes', which the author produced, about the regressions recorded by Arnall Bloxham.

Thanks are also due to various historians, psychiatrists, colleagues and researchers in various parts of Britain, France and America, most of whom are mentioned in the text.

ARNALL BLOXHAM

WHEN still a child, Arnall Bloxham became convinced that he had lived before. At the turn of the century, young Bloxham's sleep had frequently been disturbed by nightmares, dreams of past ages, people and places totally unfamiliar to him in waking hours. Later he came to believe that these dreams were scenes from a past life; that like those children more recently described by the American psychologist, Professor Ian Stevenson,* he had been born with some memory of another incarnation.

Bloxham recalled, 'Sometimes the dreams were very pleasant and others were very disturbing. And I used to wake up howling or screaming with terror when I was a boy. It was not a nice thing, to be able to remember – but, of course, I had no control over the dreams, and I used to have to get my governess or somebody to hold my hand when I went to sleep, because I was afraid of what was going to happen next.'

Much later in life, Bloxham believes he accidentally found a location he knew from his dreams, a place which had been his home in some past life – 'I was taking my aunt and step-mother around the countryside, we were in the Cotswolds, when I suddenly felt "this is the very road about which I used to dream".

'It was down a steep hill, trees on either side, and the road was yellow and very dusty – and in the dreams I always felt very ill because I was travelling in a coach which was suspended by thongs, leather thongs, which used to make the coach sway and I'd feel very seasick. And I knew that if we

---

* See Professor Stevenson's introduction to *Second Time Round* by E. W. Ryall, 1974.

went down the steep hill, turned to the right, in about half a mile or so we'd come to two towers and iron gates.

'And we did this and came to Sudeley castle and I realised that was where I had once lived – behind those iron gates.'

On that visit the castle's gates remained locked – it was not open to the public, not even to reincarnated residents. Later, Bloxham says he went again with his wife and a friend. He was able to show them around without a guide, and to lead them to an Elizabethan window which he 'knew' was there.

Young Bloxham grew up in Pershore, Worcestershire, a small country town where market gardening and plum growing were the main occupations. While still a schoolboy at Worcester Royal Grammar School, he became interested in hypnotism, referred to in those days as 'Mesmerism', and when a school friend complained of a headache, young Bloxham saw it as a chance to use his skill. He never doubted for a second it would work and it was his first success as a hypnotherapist.

Bloxham intended to become a doctor, and carried on with his study of Mesmerism, which he thought might be a useful ability for a medical man to possess. Then, when he was eighteen, the 1914–1918 war intervened and Arnall Bloxham joined the Navy and served aboard minesweepers.

But his ambitions to be a doctor collapsed. Taken ill with typhoid fever, he was assured that because he might carry infection, he could never work in a hospital.

The frustrated doctor became a hypnotherapist and, apart from naval service in both world wars, has practised the art of curing under hypnosis for more than forty years, many of them in Christchurch, New Zealand.

Bloxham finally settled in Cardiff, in South Wales, because, as a naval lieutenant in the Second World War, he was posted to the Welsh seaport. When the war ended, he stayed on and soon began to practice hypnotherapy again.

Bloxham and his second wife Dulcie made a considerable impact upon the city of Cardiff. His reputation as a hypnotherapist grew rapidly, patients were soon being referred to him by doctors and psychiatrists, he gave public lectures and appeared on television, along with a dentist and a willing patient, to demonstrate that teeth could be extracted using hypnotism as an anaesthetic.

'Gradually, there was a great change in the attitude of the medical profession towards hypnosis. It was unacceptable to them at first and doctors looked at us a bit askance. Later on, doctors would send members of their own families to me for treatment but seemed reluctant to refer ordinary patients. This I found a bit hypocritical. But nowadays hypnosis is quite accepted, is used in hospitals, and doctors have even come to me to ask if I would teach them how to hypnotise. Perhaps because of the way things were in the past, I have declined to pass on my secrets to them individually, although they were always welcome to attend my lectures.'

Today, hypnotherapy is recognised and Bloxham is President of the British Society of Hypnotherapists, in 1972 succeeding T. G. Warne-Berisford, who had formed the society in 1950.

But in Cardiff, Bloxham's reputation was founded not so much on hypnotherapy as on the interest he created in reincarnation and Eastern philosophy. To be a professional hypnotist seemed strange enough to his neighbours, but once every three weeks Bloxham opened his rambling house for about thirty friends and a sprinkling of complete strangers and held one of his 'sessions'. Dulcie Bloxham served tea and biscuits and Arnall Bloxham played tape recordings of people he had hypnotised and regressed to 'previous existences'. Afterwards, he answered questions and spoke to his audience about reincarnation and the Law of Karma.

To some he seemed a mere eccentric, but for others he was a sort of magician – Arnall and Dulcie Bloxham, in an unlikely part of the world, kindled a real interest in occult philosophy.

'I didn't perform any demonstrations of hypnosis for them – in fact I strongly disapprove of stage hypnotism and that sort of thing. It's too serious a subject and too dangerous to be used in that way; you could never be sure with a lot of people on a public stage that you had removed all the power of suggestion from their minds. There was a man who was told by a stage hypnotist he would fall asleep every time a certain tune was played – later when he heard the tune on the car radio he drove into a brick wall.

'What I did was to play tapes and explain things to people who wanted to come and listen. These sessions might have been an unorthodox way of making people think, but nothing that was any good was ever just orthodox. Nobody ever became a millionaire by being orthodox. You have to consider the orthodox and say "is that any good?" and usually the answer is "no".'

This series of meetings, unique in the social life of Cardiff, ended with the sudden death of Dulcie Bloxham. She had been Arnall Bloxham's great support, and in the 1960s had tried to get his work on regressions known to a wider audience by writing a book, *Who was Ann Ockenden?*, the story of a schoolteacher whom Bloxham had regressed to seven different 'lives', but it did not make a great impact.

Since her death, Bloxham, sometimes in failing health, has lived alone, but supported by frequent visits from a loyal band of followers from Cardiff and further afield. One good friend, a medium from the South of England, makes frequent trips to stay with the old man, sometimes arriving without warning, having packed a bag and left Weymouth in a great rush after receiving a 'psychic message' that Bloxham was not very well.

Throughout his life, Bloxham has believed in reincarnation, but his experiments with regressions to 'a past life' began only late in his career.

'It didn't start as simply an experiment, out of curiosity, because I'm a bit wary about experimenting with the mind – you wouldn't poke about with a pin in the workings of a watch, not unless you were sure what you were doing and had a good reason. But this first regression arose out of the treatment of a patient.

'I had a man who came to me because he was a hypochondriac. Professionally he was a chemist and, of course, he ought never to have been a chemist – every time he saw a label on a bottle which said "have you pains in the back?", or mentioned the symptoms of housemaid's knee, he'd say to himself: "I've got that lot!" And then he'd take his own medicines to cure these imaginary illnesses.

'When he came to see me he was in a terrible state. I wrote down a list of all the things he said he had wrong with him and I thought, "This fellow seems to have everything the matter with him that I have ever heard of."

'Anyway, I put him under hypnosis and eventually cured him of all this hypochondria. But then his wife said, "There's one thing remaining. He's terribly afraid he's going to die. Sometimes I have to cradle him in my arms at night and he'll sob like a child with the fear of death. He's afraid to go to sleep in case he won't wake up." '

Bloxham thought about his patient's problem. Unlike the cure for the imagined illnesses, he couldn't hypnotise the chemist and assure him he was not going to die! But to Bloxham the solution was simple, nevertheless.

'I told his wife – "Yes, I can cure him. I'll put him under hypnosis and make him realise that he has lived before. Therefore, if he lived before, he'll live again."

'And it worked, absolutely, his complete view of life changed. He was no longer afraid of death. You see death, as part of our western religion, doesn't seem to hold out very much hope for people who are afraid of being obliterated completely.'

Under hypnosis, the chemist told Bloxham he was the son of a sea captain, whose family moved to London in the seventeenth century. But the captain and his wife died, apparently of plague, and the son quickly married. His new problem was that he and his wife were always quarrelling, usually over the man's reluctance to work.

Bloxham told me that, during this first regression, he decided to experiment – 'I wanted to see how reliable the regression was. I wanted to know if I could encourage the man to tell me a lie.'

The hypnotist suggested to the chemist that he might have

been a highwayman. There was uncertainty for a minute and the chemist said – 'That question you asked me. I was never a highwayman, but when I was a lad we used to go to the forest and pretend to hold up people. But we didn't ever do it.'

From similar experiments with questioning techniques, Bloxham believes that although a hypnotised person can be made to fantasise, it is possible, if the hypnotist remains neutral and unobtrusive, to secure a regression that is entirely the subject's own memory of a past life.

And he believes that to become aware of a past life can be a beneficial experience.

'Most people who have been regressed find it helps them a great deal. If you can remember doing things in a previous life, well you can probably do them in this one. The past is very important – after all if you couldn't remember living yesterday, you wouldn't know very much today. And if you can't remember your previous lives, well you won't know as much as you might.

'I think all the great musicians and great artists of the past, they've perhaps been aware of having lived before and that's why they become prodigies at a very early age.'

Bloxham himself, in his younger days, was a fine natural painter. He never had any tuition and believes his ability with a paintbrush comes from knowledge gained in a previous life. A number of very stylish portraits are still at his home and strongly resemble the work of the Victorian painter Edward Burne-Jones, whose work, Bloxham says, he has never studied.

Today, the hypnotist defines himself as a Christian who believes in reincarnation and the Law of Karma – 'I think that in the course of time you reach the state of the Absolute, when you can do almost anything without having to learn in this life – you don't need to be reborn then.

'It does not matter really whether people believe in reincarnation or not. All people are reborn. It's the law of life – of birth and rebirth. And if people only asked themselves the question – "Who am I, the eternal me, who has lived before?" – then they would start remembering previous lives. But if you think that when you die you go to the grave and that's the end of you – naturally you don't contemplate the possibility of living again.

'It needs concentration, contemplation and meditation – three things that we in the west usually don't do. But if you could remember several lives, you would become almost a person of several identities; you would remember past talents and abilities learned in previous lives.

'I am actually a Christian, and of course a Christian doesn't need to believe anything particularly. One of the great things, about, say, the Church of England, is it hasn't any narrow views. You can believe anything you like. And so I believe in reincarnation.

'I also believe Christ taught reincarnation and I don't think religious Christianity today is anything like the sort of thing Christ taught. The Church of Rome started trimming it up and making it quite a different thing. You see, much of our religion is dogma – the enemy of progress and knowledge.'

Bloxham will argue strongly for his belief in reincarnation and the regressions. But he does accept that occasionally during a regression a hypnotised person appears to make a mistake when speaking about a past time. 'Some discrepancies you are bound to get, because it's only a question of memory. Even if a person is sitting a bachelor of arts examination, they can still get things wrong.'

Memory can be fallible, admits Bloxham, especially when it is cast back over hundreds of years, but errors in his regressions are not normally blamed on the hypnotised person – 'You can check these things against history, but a lot of history is written with a political pen, a bias in some direction, religious or otherwise. A lot of what you read in history is not true – I'm sure of that!'

Asked if it is possible that his hypnotised subjects are embroidering a fantasy around some forgotten historical story heard long ago, Bloxham believes he has the answer – that he can demonstrate that memory of a past life is distinct from any fund of memory normally acquired in this life.

'I have asked hypnotised people questions about a period of history which they know very well. But the answers I have had differ completely from what they've read about it in this life. If I suggest anything to them, which may be historically acceptable, but which is contrary to what is happening in their previous life, they will deny it.'

And what gives the Bloxham Tapes a true feeling of reality, insists the hypnotist, is not the cream of his collection – those regressions which can usefully be scrutinised in detail by historians – but the remainder.

'Most of my tapes are of deadly dull, ordinary people who have lived and died, having done nothing whatsoever – perhaps been housewives and nothing has ever happened. The tapes people hear about are only the highlights of my researches.'

Chapter 1

HE SAW THE EXECUTION OF CHARLES I

MY first meeting with Arnall Bloxham was in October
1974. I called at his home to see if it would be worthwhile offering the BBC a television programme about this
legendary old man.

The entire context of our meeting seemed bizarre. In a
casual conversation at a party, a woman who said she was
an astrologer – the first of her species I'd ever met – urged me
to see Bloxham. I had heard of him but I confessed he had
been so long out of the headlines, I thought he was dead.

In fact Arnall Bloxham turned out to be very much alive.
He was a small man, white haired and immaculately dressed
with a rose in his buttonhole. His features were small, almost
birdlike, with an impassivity that was quite Oriental. His voice
and manner, quiet and precise, must have inspired confidence
in his consulting room. Although nearly eighty years old he
still treated numerous patients.

In Bloxham's rather lonely old house on the outskirts of
Cardiff we were served tea by another middle-aged lady, a
friend of Bloxham's, who said she was a 'psychic medium'.
A little later, at Bloxham's rather amused bidding, she put her
hand on my forehead, closed her eyes and pronounced that in
previous incarnations I had once been a Moor and later a
French alchemist. Both lives had ended violently!

I shrugged it off. Mediums and the paraphernalia of ouija
boards and tea leaves have never fascinated me. At that stage,
I was not very optimistic that Mr Bloxham and his hypnosis
would yield me very much. My impression of the oddity of
the meeting was heightened by the setting. We sat in the
hypnotist's lounge, which has a handsome four-poster bed in

which he sleeps and on the wall, a death mask of a nobleman said to have been murdered in that same bed. His hypnotist's couch was an ancient Welsh Bardic chair in carved oak. And Bloxham himself sat alongside a small antique table, piled high with tape recordings in neatly labelled boxes.

When I asked him about them, he told me, very matter of fact, that over the previous twenty years he had tape-recorded over four hundred examples of reincarnation. Under repeated sessions of hypnosis some of his subjects had regressed to as many as fourteen quite separate existences spread out over the centuries.

Now I had done some background reading, and I thought, if Bloxham's claim is true, then his tapes are possibly the largest investigation ever recorded into this phenomenon of regression under hypnosis. If true, then that single famous case of regression, published in 1954 in *The Search for Bridey Murphy*, was just a tune on an Irish fiddle compared to his symphony of voices.

He seemed an honest and balanced man, but it was a lot to take on trust. Then, as casually as if he were telling me where people had been for their holidays, he told me of an eye-witness account of the Great Fire of London in September 1666, and about someone who had lived in the Stone Age.

He played part of a tape in which a woman relived being a victim of a massacre of Jews in York in the twelfth century. Her agonised description of violence, fire and the death of her daughter and herself was frankly hair-raising. But I accepted it as if I was listening to a very dramatic play – as yet I did not know enough about the historical background, the woman involved or Arnall Bloxham.

But one name he mentioned decided me upon a next step. He said that years before he had hypnotised and regressed a young Press photographer named John Pike. Now it happened I knew a film cameraman called John Pike, who had made some outstanding television documentaries and completed tours of duty in Vietnam and Belfast. He was back in Cardiff and was not the sort of man I imagined would be much impressed with theories of reincarnation.

A few days later I was able to sit down and talk with him. Over a drink, he still recalled clearly his visit to the hypnotist's, even though the tape-recording I subsequently listened to was dated 3 October 1957.

In his early days as a Press photographer, Pike went with a local reporter to visit Bloxham for a newspaper article about the supernatural. Bloxham, in his usual calm way, responded to their questions about reincarnation by suggesting a demonstration. First of all he hypnotised the reporter and tape-recorded a regression. And then he repeated the process with the photographer.

Pike recalled that the reporter had regressed to become a lawyer defending a country lad at an Assize court in England over a hundred years ago. The boy was found guilty of theft and sentenced to transportation. The 'lawyer' then became irritated with Bloxham's questions. First, the hypnotist was unfamiliar with the name of a noted judge of the time, and second, Bloxham apparently suggested that, because the sentence seemed harsh, the boy might appeal. 'Appeal, appeal, what is appeal?' was the angry response.

That was intriguing, because I soon found there had, in fact, never been any right of appeal under English law until the Judicature Acts of 1873. The 'lawyer' had been right.

John Pike told me he wasn't impressed by his colleague's performance. He thought, at the time, the reporter was 'putting it on'.

But when it was Pike's turn to be hypnotised, he saw pictures and recalled events that puzzle him to this day. Recorded on tape, Pike becomes a wealthy farmer living near Kidderminster. He describes the clothes of the period, coins of the time he had in his purse, and how he eventually rode to London in the year 1649. In Whitehall, perched sidesaddle on his horse, he saw over the heads of a large crowd and Roundhead soldiers, the unfolding of a great historical event – the execution of King Charles I of England.

John Pike remembers vividly that as the axe fell he shuddered and turned his eyes away.

Following this meeting with Pike, I revisited Bloxham and over a period of weeks heard, not without scepticism, tape recordings of an astonishing variety of regressions.

There was an ordinary housewife who, when hypnotised, crossed the sex barrier and, in a country accent vastly different from her own, became an illiterate farmer's boy. The highspot of the lives of these rustic lads was drinking in the local alehouse and trying to coax the barmaids to an upstairs room while the tavern keeper was face down, drunk in the sawdust.

And the rollicking description of what went on when two of the lads got upstairs with only one barmaid might have warranted a death sentence for one of 'the lads' in those far off times – rectal sex was a hanging offence in Merrie England until 1861.

Other hypnotised people wept over traumas in petty existences and there were battles relived with a ferocity and involvement that would have won awards had the roles been acted on stage.

One man who went back to a sort of Stone Age tried to describe people's appearances, insisting that he had never seen anybody with a colour of hair which might remotely fit the description 'grey'. Bloxham took this to mean that in those bad old days nobody ever lived long enough to get grey hair.

I was fascinated by it all, but still very uneasy. Was there any chance of proving even a likelihood that any of these four hundred so called 'existences' had actually happened?

I began reading books on psychology and hypnotism. I talked to psychologists about this particular form of regression under hypnosis and got a mixed reception. One admitted candidly that in real terms almost nothing is known about the inner workings of the subconscious mind – a conclusion my reading seemed to bear out.

But mostly they said the same thing – 'Ah yes. This is cryptomnesia," which means the subject has embroidered a fantasy, probably about some event they have previously read or heard of, except they have genuinely forgotten ever having had any prior knowledge of it.

One psychiatrist snapped 'cryptomnesia' at me with such brusqueness, before he had heard any of the details of the cases, that I told him he used the term with a readiness that almost amounted to panic. Our conversation got nowhere, and it was only afterwards I wished I'd suggested that perhaps some members of his profession are wary of reincarnation because they might end up with someone on their couch with fourteen separate lives to be analysed.

But they did have a point. I discovered that the reputation of Bridey Murphy, a sensation in 1954, had been much damaged by the suggestion that as a child the subject had been told a lot about life in last-century Ireland by an old lady who lived nearby, and who actually seemed to have been called Bridey Murphy.

So how was I to proceed? Clearly Bloxham's tapes could not be accepted at their face value. The answer, it seemed to me, lay with the historians: in demonstrating through them, if I could, that perhaps some of Bloxham's subjects knew things they could not have gleaned from books or stories.

Even that was going to be difficult. If you consider your own life, could you prove you existed even twenty years ago – without calling upon the evidence of friends or relatives? And what if we are talking about an age without driving licences and records of income tax?

Even if you managed to prove that someone with your name existed twenty years ago, a cynic could say you were assuming someone else's existence: that you were fantasising about someone else's life and pretending it was your own. To counter that suggestion – are you sure your knowledge of history and the life of your society of twenty years ago will convince a historian that you were alive then? Couldn't you have read what you know in a book the day before yesterday?

In those early days, pondering my self-appointed task, it almost seemed the quest was bound to be fruitless. Critics

with Western minds, very like my own, had inevitably rejected cases of this sort and often made mincemeat of so-called
investigations that pointed towards reincarnation.

I was only a little comforted to discover that, although the
notion of rebirth is alien to our western society today, it was
accepted by sections of the Church until as late as the sixth
century. Many early Christians could countenance the pros-
pect quite equably.

I was not an early Christian – not even a late one. But I
also found that many far greater minds than mine, both
eastern and western, had been believers in reincarnation –
men as varied as Napoleon, Benjamin Franklin and Henry
Ford. There was obviously much more to be said for the
idea than I imagined at the outset, and I concluded that my
belief or potential belief was unimportant. This curious
phenomenon of the Bloxham Tapes would simply have to
be investigated to the full, and the outcome would speak for
itself.

Chapter 2

A COLLEAGUE IN ANCIENT GREECE

M Y first task with the Bloxham Tapes was a weeding-out process, to discard those tapes I felt could not be researched or proven. To listen to the full collection would take something like a thousand hours – to research them all would take years.

But I needn't have worried. The vast majority were of ordinary humdrum lives, stories from the past but incapable of any sort of objective proof. It was interesting that if what the psychiatrists said was true, and people were fantasising about themselves, then most were pitching their fantasies modestly and surprisingly low.

Most of the so-called previous lives were in fact so ordinary the hypnotist himself became bored with them long before his twenty years of research was completed. Latterly Bloxham would hypnotise and regress only people in whom he sensed the possibility of an interesting or unusual regression.

I though about being hypnotised myself to see if that would prove anything, but rejected the idea, suspecting, rightly or wrongly, that researches into the work of a hypnotist by a man he had hypnotised would lack credibility. I would be fascinated to try it later.

But I needed some objective proof of the existence of this phenomenon. And soon after my first meeting with Bloxham I went along with a colleague, Beata Lipman, who was prepared to be hypnotised for the first time. To my amazement she regressed instantly and described a life as a farmer's daughter in Ancient Greece. She had to be woken up smartly when she went into an imaginary but very real labour for a child she thought she was bearing by her Ancient Greek husband named Artemius.

This lady has never been to Greece nor taken any interest in Greek history. Historically, she had always thought the Greeks 'a very dull lot'.

This was the first time I had seen Bloxham work and there were absolutely no leading questions either before or during the session. He simply invited the subject, when hypnotised, to 'go back in time' . . . and back she went.

Afterwards, she told me of a series of pictures and images of herself which so astonished her she was not able fully to describe them for the hypnotist. She had thoughts and sensations unlike any she has experienced, but was aware throughout of the existence of Bloxham and the twentieth century and mentally cancelled out some of the new facts that came to her because they seemed 'so far-fetched'.

Gradually, I concentrated my researches upon a limited number of the Bloxham tapes where it seemed to me the details coincided remarkably with known but quite obscure periods of history. Regressions too in which people talked about cities or countries they had apparently never visited in their present lives.

In some cases they made statements contrary to the current teachings of history. And yet historians usually could not say their versions were wrong, because they appeared to be talking about gaps in our present knowledge – much to the surprise of some eminent professors of history.

There were other people too whose regressions I found fascinating for very different reasons. Sometimes quite cultured men and women became illiterate and uncouth under hypnosis. In unrecognisable voices they displayed a knowledge of slang, archaic terms and a general familiarity with life in the gutter of a bygone age that was simply astounding.

In one case I was not the first person to be impressed. This concerned an educated Swansea man who regressed two hundred years and in a coarse west country accent described the squalor and horror of life as a pressed man aboard a thirty-two-gun frigate in the British Navy.

Bloxham told me that Lord Louis Mountbatten, former First Lord of the Admiralty, had a copy of this tape 'on permanent loan'. Researches and the opinions of some of Britain's finest naval historians dropped into my lap as a result of Earl Mountbatten's interest.

He had been so fascinated by the tape that he had had his nephew, Prince Philip, and some other top naval men try to trace the ship in which the 'gunner's mate' was serving in an action against the French off the coast of Calais around the year 1800.

I also followed up this man's account – one of the most gripping narratives I have ever heard – in which he ends up apparently with his leg shattered by a ball from a French ship.

After I had made my selection of tapes, it was interesting to find a high percentage, like the gunner's mate tape – chosen really because they were so detailed and graphically recalled – ending in violence or sudden death.

Interesting, because I immediately came across some words written by one of the world's leading authorities on the controversial evidence for reincarnation. Dr Ian Stevenson MD of the University of Virginia, wrote: 'Violent death ends the life of the previous personality in from forty to eighty percent of the Asian cases. The incidence varies from one culture to another . . . we all tend to remember best what moved us most. Quite so. So why should not this law of the mind apply equally well to memories of previous lives in the minds of those who have them? I have come, indeed, to count this feature as an indication of the authenticity of a case. . . .'

But this initial weeding-out process was not a story of one illuminating discovery after another. Of all Bloxham's cases only one appeared to be what might be called an 'historical celebrity'. And even one seemed to me rather too many. After all, in a random selection of four hundred people, there are unlikely to be any celebrities – and especially one as famous as Queen Elizabeth I of England.

As I listened to the tape, I noted that the lady did not appear to undergo any real change of voice or personality in the way the others did. And she also seemed to think it was she, as 'Queen Elizabeth', who had caused Sir Walter Raleigh to be beheaded. In fact, it was Elizabeth's successor – James I.

Sadly, I abandoned her regression, writing it off as cryptomnesia plus inadequate reading. Sad, because she added spice to history with an account of the Virgin Queen making love with Sir Walter in the cabin of his ship.

At first this example disturbed me. Did it mean the other tapes were equally suspect? But as I read more about psychology and hypnotism, and watched Bloxham regressing other people, sometimes for the first time, I realised the hypnotist has virtually no control over whether the voice, appearing to speak from the past, is genuinely from the past and not from the imagination. One bad apple had no significance for the other three hundred and ninety-nine. They could be quite different, but it was up to me to try to prove it.

Chapter 3

JANE EVANS HAS SEVEN LIVES

I BEGAN work upon what proved to be the most consistently astonishing case in Bloxham's collection: a woman who had regressed to six quite separate lives. Adding her present-day existence as a married woman in her late thirties, working in an office, she could talk lucidly about seven identities.

Initially I was impressed because the first three tapes I listened to dealt with periods of history well outside the knowledge of most of us. Yet the facts, as I began to check them off, kept falling into place. Many of the details she gave I was unable to believe until I had consulted history books and historians. And the answer was nearly always the same: 'true' or 'could well be true'.

There were even a few instances where historians at first said: 'No, this is not so.' But after further researches they called me up to say they had changed their minds.

Satisfied there was something to go on, I asked Bloxham to arrange a meeting with this lady. She turned out to be a lively, intelligent young woman. I learned we had both attended the same High School at Newport in Monmouthshire, but I was a few years older and neither of us recalled ever meeting the other.

My knowledge of the school enabled me to check a few more facts. I'd wondered if the basic outline of the three lives, which had impressed me so much, could have been gleaned from an advanced study of history or perhaps even of French or Latin at school. But the relevant periods of history were not on the syllabus in her time, and she never studied history, French or Latin to an advanced level. She dropped all three

subjects after her Ordinary Level examinations at the age of
sixteen and soon left school altogether to take a secretarial
course at a business college.

The three lives in question apparently took place in the
Roman British City of Eboracum or York in the third century;
again in York as a Jewess at the time of the massacre of 1190;
and at Bourges in France as a servant to the French merchant
prince Jacques Coeur in the fifteenth century.

She claimed she had no recollection of ever reading anything of the history of these particular places, and she had
never set foot in either York or Bourges. Her total experience
of France was a two-day stay in Paris on her way back from
the World Fair in Brussels in 1958. And Paris is remote from
Bourges in the Loire Valley.

Despite this apparent unfamiliarity with both locations she
named streets and places in York when regressing as the
Jewess, and, in the French regression, gave a detailed account
of the interior of Jacques Coeur's sumptuous house at Bourges,
which I later visited to check for myself.

To complete the tally of this lady's rather startling past,
were three regressions – as a Spanish handmaiden in the time
of Catherine of Aragon in the sixteenth century; as a poor
little sewing girl in the London of the reign of Queen Anne
in the early seventeenth century; and as a nun in a convent in
Maryland, USA, at the turn of the present century.

It was a formidable and fascinating list. None of the lives
overlapped, and the smallest interval between them appeared
to be something like fifteen years – from the death of the nun
to her present date of birth in 1939.

Neither she nor Bloxham suggested the list might be comprehensive. It was simply that after six regressions, she became 'a bit fed up and frightened by it all', and refused to
do any more.

It was, she said, very tiring – at least two of the lives end
in violent death – and after a session recording the latest of
these, she walked out of Bloxham's consulting room and

fainted. For the next few days she felt unwell, and eventually her husband insisted she do no more.

When I spoke to her, it was over five years since she had last been hypnotised. I asked why she had been hypnotised in the first place – the explanation was fairly straightforward. Driving with her husband in Cardiff, she saw a poster about Bloxham the hypnotherapist: 'Arnall Bloxham says rheumatism is psychological.'

Having suffered earlier in life from rheumatoid arthritis, she said rather crossly that she'd like to meet any hypnotist who believed he could cure rheumatism. Her husband took her at her word, and, through a mutual friend, arranged to meet Arnall Bloxham and his wife Dulcie, who was alive at that time.

Over tea, she told Bloxham that her interests included reading about Greece and Tibet – but she couldn't explain what fascinated her about these countries.

That was enough for Bloxham, and sensing a possible interesting regression to one of these countries, he asked if she would be hypnotised. He got his interesting regression all right – but although he tried on six occasions, Bloxham's new subject never uttered a word about either Greece or Tibet!

Wondering still if there was not some very straightforward explanation for her knowledge of Roman Britain, medieval French politics, and life as a Jewess, I asked if her family had encouraged her to read books about such subjects or perhaps told her stories about them.

She laughed – her father had been a boy soldier who ran away from home in Rotherham to escape the family tradition of becoming a coalminer. In the army he was quickly posted to South Wales and still lives there. He was not a man who read books, she said, and he knew nothing about history. Nor had she absorbed these stories from her mother who had been equally uninterested in such topics.

As for once being a Jewess, all she could connect was a grandmother who was said to be 'Jewish'. This lady had died when her grand-daughter was aged six. The two had never lived together, and she could not recall they had ever met. Her father had been known to say that this good woman was possibly 'more gypsy than Jewess', and she sounded an unlikely source for history lessons about the Jews of Medieval England.

These queries disposed of, I asked if she would be prepared to be hypnotised and regressed once again. Only this time I wanted to be present with a film camera as well as a tape-recorder.

She thought it over for a few days and then telephoned me to agree. But there was one condition. I could film her under hypnosis, but not publish her real name. Her husband, in particular, wanted a minimum of attention focused upon the fact that his wife appeared to have had seven lives.

It seemed a reasonable request, and 'Jane Evans', as anonymous a name as I could think of, became her new title.

The six regressions of Jane Evans, with appropriate dates, are:

Tutor's wife in Roman Britain AD 286.
Jewess in York, died 1190.
Servant to Jacques Coeur, died 1451.
Servant to Catherine of Aragon, who lived 1485–1536.
Lonon sewing girl in the reign of Queen Anne, who lived from 1665–1714.
Nun in Maryland, USA, died 1920 approx.
Jane Evans born in 1939.

Chapter 4

A TWELFTH-CENTURY JEWESS

IN the first Bloxham tape I'd heard, Jane Evans is hypnotised and becomes Rebecca. She begins with a description of the exterior of York Minster – or, as she calls it, the cathedral of York. Rebecca, the Jewess, is in the nearby market place buying fruit and vegetables. The date is 'the Christian year of 1189'.

Her husband, she says, is 'Joseph of the seed of Ezekiel', a wealthy moneylender. Rebecca and Joseph are both aged forty and have two children: an eighteen-year-old son Joseph who helps in his father's business, and Rachel who is eleven.

The family live in a fairly large stone house – 'three big rooms downstairs and five upstairs' – to the north of the City, an area of York where Rebecca says most of the wealthy Jews live.

Now the history of this time is far from precise. Little more than the names of a handful of Jews from this community are known to us, and it had not been thought this particular Jewish community lived to the north of the city, although there is no real evidence to the contrary. Today in York there is a municipal car park covering an area known as Jewbury, which was certainly the burial ground of the medieval Jewish community from 1230, a mere forty years on. Jewbury is certainly to the north – to be precise the north-east – so it is quite feasible that the preceding community also lived in that part of the City.

As to Rebecca's origins, she says that her 'father's father' came to York from Cyprus but 'although born here we are not English – we are outcasts' – a point she amplifies when describing the clothes worn by her husband:

B

Rebecca: He wears robes. Costly robes, but they have to look as if they are not costly robes. We are despised for our wealth. They covet our houses and we all have to wear yellow badges, circles over our hearts, to show that we are Jewish.

Bloxham: Do you mind having to wear these circles?

Rebecca: Yes.

Bloxham: Do you?

Rebecca: Yes. They mock us because of our religion. They mock us because we cleanse ourselves, because we teach our sons, because we won't eat unclean food. They mock us. They make us wear these patches on our clothes to show that we are Jews.

Now it is a fact that from the year 1215 every Jew in Christendom was compelled, on papal authority, to wear a badge signifying he was a Jew. But could the wearing of such a badge have been imposed earlier? Professor Barrie Dobson of York University, an authority on Jewish history of this period, assures me it could: 'It is quite conceivable that in parts of England or in the whole of England some sort of badge of the sort she mentions might have been imposed on York Jews in the late twelfth century.' But Rebecca and her family had more to worry them than the indignity of being forced to wear a badge:

Bloxham: Are you happy yourself?

Rebecca: We are happy as a family but we are worried. We are nervous because of the uprisings in Chester and in London and Lincoln against the Jews.

References exist to anti-Jewish risings in London, Lincoln and Colchester, amongst others, so was Rebecca confusing Chester with Colchester or was there a separate incident in that city?

Bloxham: Why is there an uprising?

Rebecca: They always hate us – they've always hated us. Between Pentecost and Passover, pestilence visited the city of York – two hundred Christians died – no Jews died. And they blame us. They blame us. (*Pause.*)
They borrow our money – where would they be if it were not for the Jews? They borrow our money to build their cathedrals and finance the wars in Ireland. Where would they be without their Jews?
Bloxham: Are there wars in Ireland?
Rebecca: This was two, three years ago – they borrowed money from the Jews to finance the wars. What else can we do but lend money?

It is almost certain that King Henry II borrowed money from the Jewish money-lending community to finance his expeditions in Ireland. He had annexed that country in 1171 but was plagued by insurrections, and certainly in the mid-1180s had sent another costly expedition under the command of his son Prince John.

Bloxham: Who is the king who borrowed this money?
Rebecca: Henry Plantagenet (*pause*); he is a good king. He is good to the Jews. He helps us when we have to take our cases to the courts for the money that is owed us. In return we give him ten (*pause*) ten parts of the money that we gather back.
Bloxham: Have you ever seen the king?
Rebecca: No.

This too seems to present a quite accurate picture of King Henry of the House of Plantagenet and his relations with the Jews. They were certainly given protection in his courts and it is known that the king exacted a payment for this. But Rebecca is speaking in the year of Henry's death and already forces are building up within this medieval society that will soon have a tragic consequence for the Jews of York.

Bloxham: Have you a synagogue?

Rebecca: Yes.

Bloxham: Perhaps it's a small one?

Rebecca: Yes, they do not allow us very much. We are not recognised by them at all. (*Pause and then angrily.*) They take our money but they do not recognise us at all. A Jew is not allowed to enter the army or hold land under feudal tenure, so what else can we do but lend money. We are not allowed to enter the army or go into trade, what else can we do?

Bloxham: So none of the Jews are in trade there?

Rebecca: Pedlars not tradesmen.

Bloxham: Have there been any happenings lately?

Rebecca: Yes. A priest from the Christian Pope came, asking – came to the market place – asking men to sew crosses on to their robes and go to fight the infidels who have taken Jerusalem. And he told them to raise up their arms against the infidels and to join the armies – to join the armies in the Holy Land.

Bloxham: Did you see this representative of the Pope?

Rebecca: Yes.

Bloxham: What was he like?

Rebecca: Just a priest.

Bloxham: Do you know his name?

Rebecca: Massotti (*pause*) Massotti – And when he said 'take up your arms against the infidels', the people in the crowd said 'what about the infidels in York, all Jews are infidels.' And we are frightened, we are frightened. (*Pause.*) My husband has sent money out of York to our uncle in Lincoln in case something terrible happens. King Henry is good to us, but King Henry is getting old – where would we be if it were anyone but Henry?

Bloxham: Do you know what men are going to the Holy Land to fight against the infidels?

Rebecca: No, only the men from the town. I think they are going just for the money and probably to get away from their wives.

Bloxham: Do you think they want to get away from their wives?

Rebecca: Yes, they are not so close in their families as we are. They have no family life as we have.

In fact, Rebecca seems to be describing events leading up to the Third Crusade, which would be under way within a year, after two years of preparation, and with the next King of England, Richard Coeur de Lion, at its head. Historically, it is known that anti-Jewish as well as anti-Moslem feeling was being whipped up. A mass hysteria about 'the infidels' was sweeping France and England and there were numerous riots and killings. Jews were seen as 'enemies of Christ', and the Pope himself, in writing, warned Englishmen of their 'corrupting influence on Christian souls'. Priests certainly took part in the tub-thumping that led up to the Third Crusade, but whether a priest called Massotti was one of the rabble rousers who came to York, I have been unable to discover.

Another intriguing point is Rebecca's reference to sending money to 'our uncle in Lincoln'. There were certainly close ties between the Jewish money-lending communities of York and Lincoln, so much so that Professor Dobson in his 'The Jews of Medieval York and the Massacre of March, 1190' suggests that the York business community may have originated as an offshoot of the money-lending activities of one 'Aaron of Lincoln'.

In his paper—published in 1974, some years after Rebecca's regression—Professor Dobson allows us to conjecture even further. He refers specifically to the known close ties between the Lincoln Jews and a leader of the York community, Joseph or 'Josce' of York, a wealthy moneylender:

Josce's name is first mentioned in an undated Jewish bond or starr of Aaron of Lincoln. . . . For reasons already discussed, it seems entirely appropriate that this earliest indisputable reference to money-lending by a York Jew should occur in a document that makes clear that Jew's financial subordination to Aaron of Lincoln. Nevertheless in the following year (1176–7) Josce of York stands revealed as an important financier in his own right. . . .

So could this Joseph of York be Rebecca's husband? Forty years old in 1189, he could well have been money-lending in his late twenties, at the date given by Professor Dobson. At first a reference in the *Jewish Encyclopaedia* seemed to rule this out. There is a mention of Joseph's wife, as 'Hannah', and a reference to him being survived by 'a son Aaron who later became the Chief Rabbi in the kingdom during the reign of Henry III'.

But these family particulars are more than suspect. Joseph did not have a son named Aaron. Professor Dobson writes: 'Far from being, as is usually thought, the son of the Josce of York who had been martyred in March, 1190, the great Aaron de Ebraco himself had moved to the city from Lincoln several years after the massacre.'

In fact, other historians have confirmed that Aaron was 'son of Josce' but not 'Josce of York'. So perhaps 'Josce of York' was Rebecca's husband after all.

However, Joseph was not an uncommon name for a Jew, and Rebecca's husband could equally well be supposed to be some other member of the quite large York community.

Bloxham: Who are the important people around York?

Rebecca: I don't know.

Bloxham: Who are said to be important? You must have heard your husband talk about them?

Rebecca: Only Jewish people. (*Pause.*) There was a man called Mabelise.

Bloxham: What was his name?

Rebecca: Mabelise—he owed my husband money and we had to take him to the Assizes to get money back. And we won our case.

Bloxham: What did Mabelise do?

Rebecca (*vehemently*): Mabelise. He hates us even more.

They all hate us. (*Pause.*) We have fortified – we have fortified our windows and our doors and our courtyard doors. And we are always on watch. (*Pause.*) Some of us have even taken off our yellow patches and go about the city at night to collect our debts, because we are frightened.

Bloxham: What did this man do for a living, who borrowed money from you?

Rebecca: Mabelise?

Bloxham: Was he a trader?

Rebecca: No. He's a young man. He just wanted money and my husband let him have the money, but he would not pay us back.

Here Rebecca appears to be talking about a man labelled by chroniclers at the time of the York Massacre as 'the arch-conspirator against the Jews' – one Richard Malebisse, a name almost identical with Rebecca's 'Mabelise'.

This man was subsequently fined and banished for his role in the massacre of the Jews. It is stated that this minor nobleman of York had been in debt to them and was so unwilling to make repayments that he attempted to erase his debts by murdering his creditors.

Rebecca's husband Joseph may not conclusively be a reference to 'Josce of York' but there is little doubt her 'Mabelise' was a hated nobleman, referred to by the medieval chronicler, William of Newburgh, as 'Richard rightly called Mala Bestia' or 'evil beast'.

Today the name of Malebisse survives in the nearby Yorkshire village of Acaster Malbis, and in the twelfth century, the Jews of York had much to fear from him and others of the same mind:

Bloxham: Now this is a little later. What are you doing now?

Rebecca: We are busy packing – packing all our things in case we have to go – in case we have to go.

Bloxham: Do you think you will have to go?

Rebecca: Yes, all of us are fortifying our houses but we won't last long. We'll have to go, we'll have to flee from York.

Bloxham: And go to Lincoln?

Rebecca: We will try London, we will try. But Benjamin has told us that his father was killed in London – was murdered in London so we do not know what to do. We will try London.

Bloxham: Who is Benjamin?

Rebecca: Benjamin is in the house alongside us.

Bloxham: But aren't the people going to the Holy Land to fight rather than attack you in York?

This question seems to bear out Bloxham's admission that at this stage he had never heard of the York Massacre.

Rebecca: Yes, but it all stirs it up. It stirs up the trouble and now that Henry has died. . . .

Bloxham (*interrupting*): Henry has died?

Rebecca: Now that good King Henry has died, King Richard is away. King Richard is in the Crusades with them – who is going to help us now? We are under nobody's protection. For thirty years we were protected by Henry and now we have no one to protect us.

Bloxham: What year is this then?

Rebecca: 1189.

Bloxham: Do you want to leave York?

Rebecca: No, I do not want to leave my house, but so many awful things have happened. My husband will not tell me a lot of them, but I hear whispers about what has happened to some Jews. An old Jew called Isaac in Coney Street, he was murdered – he was murdered. Before they murdered him they made him eat pork and they poured holy water on his head and then they murdered him. And we are frightened of what they will do to us and our children. We will have to leave.

It is clear that Rebecca, as instructed by Bloxham, has moved her story on to later in the year 1189, probably October or November. For one thing, King Henry is dead (6 July) and Richard is already crowned (3 September) and is immediately off to the Crusades. And Henry's reign did last approximately thirty years, from 1154 to 1189, as Rebecca said.

It is known too there was a murder of a Jew living in Coney Street, but there is no detail. However, the interesting reference is to Benjamin who lives next door and whose father was 'murdered in London'.

History is silent about Benjamin, but it does record that a wealthy Jew from York, Benedict, a close associate of Josce of York, was attacked during an anti-Jewish riot in London, while attending the coronation of Richard at Westminster in September. Thirty Jews were killed and Benedict was so badly wounded that he died at Northampton on his return journey to York.

Benedict certainly had 'sons', as the chroniclers have recorded. Was Benjamin, who lived next door, one of these?

And the York house of Benedict, in which it is conceivable that Benjamin lived, is mentioned by the chroniclers when they describe the actual start of the York massacre in the spring of the following year, 1190. This is how Professor Dobson described it, some years after the regression was recorded:

> One stormy night, probably at the beginning of March, a band of armed conspirators took advantage of the confusion caused by a fire they may themselves have started, to break into the York house of the recently deceased Benedict. After killing all its inhabitants, including Benedict's widow and children, they set the roof afire and carried off the treasure they found there.

Compare that account with the start of the highly dramatic climax to Rebecca's own story; which also accurately suggests that the Jews sought sanctuary in the Castle of York:

Bloxham: Now this is later. Did you have to leave?

Rebecca: Yes. Yes we all had to go. They came to the house of Benjamin next to us and we could hear the screams and smell the smoke. And we had to go. My husband and our son carrying money on their back in sacks – we had to go – we fled. (*Pause*.) We wanted to go to the castle – we went through the back way to get to the castle but they were pursuing us so my husband slit a sack of silver and let it pour into the road so the people pursuing us would stop pursuing us and pick up the silver so that we could get a bit ahead of them. But we could hear screams and could smell the burning coming from the people. It was terrible. (*Very agitated*.)

And when we got to the castle, they wouldn't let us in – and they wouldn't let us in except just inside the wall – but they wouldn't give us shelter and all the people crowded outside shouting to us to come out and – shouting to us to come out – and oh – terrible. Shouting and screaming at us.

Bloxham: What did they shout?

Rebecca: Asking – telling us to come out and be killed. We were infidels, and asking if we had crucified any little boys and awful things – terrible things they were shouting at us.

Allegations that Jews indulged in ritual killing of small boys was a common feature of anti-Semitism at this time, and three 'boy martyrs' were actually declared Saints in England on the basis of such generally unfounded accusations.

And they wouldn't let us any further into the castle – we were just there and they were threatening to kill us and they were shouting out – 'two silver pieces to anyone who kills a Jew, two silver pieces to anyone who kills a Jew.' And we – they started to ram the gates and we were all just inside and they wouldn't let us any further and so people started to kill their own children rather than let them get their children.

Bloxham: Did they?

This sort of 'mercy' killing was one of the most poignant features of the York Massacre.

Rebecca (*very distressed*): Terrible – terrible – they wouldn't let us in – they promised they'd let us in and they wouldn't let us in farther than just inside the gates.

The final scenes of the massacre certainly took place within the main keep of the castle, although it is possible that, since the siege lasted several days, the early stages might have been 'just inside the gates' as described. This would also explain why the Jews so mistrusted the Constable of the castle that once he left 'on business' they refused to re-admit him to his own castle. Historians have been unable to account for this strange lock-out and lack of trust.

Bloxham: Is Rachel with you?

Rebecca: Yes and my son. And we managed to get out – somebody helped us – somebody my husband paid to help us. We got out of the castle and we took shelter in a Christian Church and we – there was a priest and a clerk in this church and we held them and bound them and told them we wouldn't hurt them as long as they didn't tell people we were there – and we were down in the cellars – down below the church – and we were so hungry and we had to eat – all we could find was wine and they called us infidels and Jewish pigs for drinking the wine – it was sacrificial wine – and we had to drink – we were thirsty – we were thirsty and hungry. And we are all here, we can hear the screams – terrible things. And the priest told us that there had been riots in London and Chester and that Jews were being killed. And John had ordered that all Jews be killed – all Jews be killed.

Bloxham: Oh dear! But you will be all right won't you?

Rebecca: We are hiding. We are cold. We are hungry. It's damp and we can hear and see from the top of the church – we can see flames coming from the – just outside the gates, the gates, the big gates outside York.

Bloxham: You are not in the church now?

Rebecca: The church is just outside the big gates and we're hoping that they won't think we're there – that they won't think that we're there. (*Pause.*) We've lost all our money.

Bloxham: How did you lose it all?

Rebecca: We have had to give most of it away to get out of the castle.

Bloxham: They won't be worried about you now will they, if they don't think you are wealthy?

Rebecca: They still hate us.

Bloxham: Do they?

Rebecca: They still hate us because we do not believe in their beliefs. (*Voice full of stress, and in a desperate situation she casts around for a crumb of comfort and debates aloud the possibilities.*) . . . But we are in their church and God's house is still God's house – but if they find us here they will surely kill us. But we must shelter – my husband is tired, his leg is wounded and injured – we must rest – we are hungry.

Bloxham: But you'll have sanctuary in the church won't you?

Rebecca: Not in the church of the Christians – they do not want us in here – they have told us we must go but we have them tied up so that they can't get away – we have told them we won't harm them.

Bloxham: How many are in there beside you and your family?

Rebecca: Only us.

Bloxham: And how did you manage to tie up the other two?

Rebecca: My husband and my son – we tied them up.

Bloxham: What is happening now?

Rebecca (*panicky voice*): We can still hear them coming –
we can see the flames – from the top of the church we
can see the flames.

Bloxham: Oh you are on the top of the church now?

Rebecca: We can see from the top of the church but we are
inside – and we can hear them coming.

Bloxham: What particular church was this?

Rebecca: It was dark, we just took refuge.

Bloxham: It was not York Minster was it?

Rebecca: No, no – just a small church outside the gates of
York (*voice distant as if responding to questions with
difficulty*), outside the big copper gate, the big copper gate
of York, copper gate of York (*voice fades then resumes in
increasing agitation and hysteria*). We can hear them –
still hear them screaming and we're frightened – Rachel
is crying – my husband has gone to see if he can find
food for us – he's gone to see if he can get food and my
son has gone with him – and we're hidden in the church
but we can still hear them – we're waiting for my son to
return – he hasn't come yet – he hasn't come yet – we
can hear the noises coming, we can hear horses. Horses
coming nearer and nearer – nearer.

Bloxham: I expect your son and husband will be back
soon?

Rebecca: Yes they must be back, they must be back, we're
worried, we're frightened – we can hear them coming,
we can hear the horses coming, we can hear the screaming and the shouting and the crying – 'burn the Jews,
burn the Jews, burn the Jews'. (*Pause.*) Where is Joseph?
Why doesn't he come back, why doesn't he come back?
(*Pause then almost screams.*) Oh God – they're coming –
they – they are coming – Rachel's crying – don't cry –
don't cry – don't cry. (*Pause.*) Aah, they've entered the
church – we can hear them – they've entered the church
– the priest is loose – the priest has got free – he has told
them we are here – they're coming – they're coming

down – the priest is free and they're coming down. (*Pause and voice almost incoherent with terror.*) Oh not – not not not Rachel! No don't take her – don't – stop – they're going to kill her – they – don't – not Rachel, no, no, no, no – not Rachel – oh, don't take Rachel – no don't take Rachel – no, no, no, no, no don't take Rachel – no.

Bloxham (*shocked*): They're not going to take her are they?

Rebecca (*grief-stricken voice*): They've taken Rachel – they've taken Rachel. . . .

Bloxham: They are not going to harm you are they? (*Silence.*)

Bloxham: Are you all right? They have left you alone have they?

Rebecca: Dark . . . dark.

Bloxham then wakes his subject.

Chapter 5

A CHURCH WITH A CRYPT

I DECIDED to take the Rebecca tape-recordings up to York to play for Professor Dobson. Also I would compare her account of the streets and buildings of twelfth-century York with what today remains of the medieval city.

But there was one task I undertook first – to film Rebecca being regressed under hypnosis. Upon this would depend whether or not we attempted to make a television film about Bloxham's work.

On the morning we set up in his consulting room, I very much doubted our chances of success. There were six of us in the television team, and I was sure that our presence, plus those intimidating lights and the camera, would make it impossible for the woman even to be hypnotised.

Not a bit – she seemed a little nervous but smiled, shook hands with everyone and settled down on Bloxham's couch. Within a minute of Bloxham speaking, she was in a trance.

This time, to give us specifically the regression as Rebecca, Bloxham varied his normal technique. Instead of telling her, quite generally, that she was going 'back, back in time', he instructed her to go back to her life in York.

Soon the deep, regular breathing was broken, at first haltingly, by the voice of Rebecca the Jewess. Under instruction, she returned to the market place and gave a rather fuller description than previously of the exterior of York Cathedral – again quite accurately.

The story seems basically the same as before – if anything it was less detailed. This was almost reassuring, because any injection of obviously new facts would perhaps have indicated she had been reading up on the York massacre. She assured me, she had read nothing about it either before or since the original regression.

On another occasion, filming a second of her recorded 'lives', I wrote some questions of my own and handed them to Bloxham during the regression. But this first time, I was anxious simply to record the pair of them, without any obvious interference from me.

Of course, there were minor additions as well as omissions from the first hypnosis as the Jewess. Bloxham asked about the accession to the throne of King Richard, after Rebecca had referred to the death of Henry Plantagenet.

Bloxham: Has that (Richard's accession) affected you at all?

Rebecca (*impatiently*): Of course it affects us – it affects us!

His brother is Archbishop, is Archbishop of York. Him! We were safe with Henry but now we must go.

This was a clear reference to what historians have termed the 'somewhat controversial' decision of Richard in August 1189 to 'elect' his illegitimate half-brother Geoffrey to the vacant see of York after an interval of ten years in which there had been no archbishop.

But more striking than the variations between Rebecca's first and second accounts of medieval York, was the disparity in temperament and manner between Rebecca the Jewess and the friendly South Wales woman who had earlier been chatting with us. The others later confirmed my impression that Rebecca the Jewess seemed altogether a more aloof person, a lady of no little dignity, who was sometimes irritated by Bloxham's probings.

'Questions, questions! So many questions, man! I'm trying, I'm trying,' she told him. Later, she seemed positively insulted:

Bloxham: How do you wash your clothes?
Rebecca (*shocked voice*): I do not wash clothes!
Bloxham: You do not wash clothes?
Rebecca: No! (*Pause.*) Wash clothes!
Bloxham: Do your servants do that?
Rebecca: Yes. (*With great finality.*)

It seemed to all of us that the Jewess was a different sort of person to the woman from Cardiff. Everyone was gripped by the power of her story and the filmed footage was capturing an intensity of emotion I had previously seen only professional actors able to reproduce before a camera. And then it happened – an incredible anti-climax.

Rebecca was describing how she and her child were down in the crypt of the church. The soldiers had entered and were about to come down – she was whispering, almost praying: 'pass us, pass us, pass us – pass by. No. They've stopped. I can hear them – they know we are here.'

Her voice was full of terror – you could have heard a pin drop in Bloxham's consulting room. Then Bloxham, presumably anxious to have Rebecca repeat that her husband and son were out foraging for food, asked 'are you hungry?' And he followed this question by asking when she had eaten last.

Rebecca's only reply was a distracted 'can't remember, can't remember'. Her face was so agitated that she was clearly re-living in her mind her last moments in the crypt, and by the time Bloxham got back to the narrative, all was 'dark'.

Rebecca of York had died quietly in her mind without telling the camera a word about it, simply because she was asked a wrong question at the crucial time. It was extremely disappointing, but at least Rebecca was not 'putting on a show' for the camera.

A few weeks later, one Sunday night in a York hotel room, I played the tapes for Professor Barrie Dobson, Reader in His-

tory at the University of York, and gave him transcripts to
take away and study.

Waiting for his verdict, I read his recently published work
on the massacre of the Jews in 1190. It seemed that Rebecca
had not centred her story around the best known historical
facts – the unfolding drama in the castle, where the Jews
sheltered from the howling mob which roamed the streets,
killing and looting.

The Jews, perhaps mistakenly, refused to allow the Royal
Constable to re-enter his own castle. He appealed for help to
the Sheriff of Yorkshire, John Marshall, who made 'the im-
petuous decision to eject the Jews from the castle by force',
using soldiers under his command.

The soldiers joined the mob, who clearly felt the presence
of troops was the king's sanction for their murderous activities. William of Newburgh, writing at the time, said 'many
milites' as well as the men of the town now felt they had a
royal warrant for killing Jews.

In her filmed regression, Rebecca specified that it was
'soldiers' who entered the church where she was in hiding.
The widespread notion that the killings were royally sanctioned is reflected when she said: 'the priest told us "Jews are
being killed, John has ordered that all Jews be killed". . . .'

According to the chroniclers, the mob was also goaded into
a 'religious frenzy' by a white-robed monk, parading up and
down the walls. Perhaps with some justice, he became the
only Christian casualty – killed by a stone rolled down from
inside the castle.

On Friday, 16 March the Jews, realising the position was
hopeless, made a pact amongst themselves. Men cut the throats
of their wives and children and in turn killed each other.
Finally, of those who had agreed to this solution, it is said
that only two were left: Josce of York and the chief rabbi
Yomtob. The rabbi then killed Josce and stabbed himself, having agreed that he alone would take upon himself the sin of
suicide.

Rebecca had mentioned that the Jews in the castle had

begun killing their own children, but if her husband Joseph is to be the same man as Josce of York, then clearly, either surviving accounts of the massacre are at fault, or more likely Josce simply returned to the castle after discovering his wife and daughter had been killed in the church.

Historically, the horror did not end there. The Jews had made a huge fire of their possessions and this spread to the wooden walls of the castle. In the morning, those Jews who survived were persuaded to come out, on the promise their lives would be spared if they accepted Christian baptism.

But the offer was false, and the survivors of the night were massacred too. The chroniclers estimated that altogether about a hundred and fifty Jews were slaughtered in the riots at York.

There was some retribution. A royal force was assembled in London and marched north. Most of the ringleaders fled – Malebisse hurried to Scotland. Both the Sheriff of Yorkshire and the Constable of the Castle were dismissed and replaced. Heavy fines were imposed on the citizens of York and a hundred hostages were taken back to London as security for the future good behaviour of the city.

Well, that was the historical version, but what did Professor Dobson have to say about Rebecca's story? His first comment was that, although Rebecca's language was more of the twentieth century than medieval England, the story was 'true to what we know of the events and the times themselves'.

Much of the detail he found 'impressively accurate' and some disputed points 'could well have been true'. A few aspects, he thought, would have been known only to professional historians.

But the professor raised a few topographical queries. The murder of an old Jew in Coney Street, as described by Rebecca, was factually acceptable. But in old records of the city, today's Coney Street was still written 'Cuninga Street', or King Street, until the end of the Middle Ages.

So why hadn't Rebecca called it 'Cuninga Street'? Does this discrepancy inevitably mean she has used a name not in existence in the late twelfth century? Not necessarily, for the written change was perhaps merely the final acknowledgement that everyone had long since stopped using the old name. Perhaps the rather pompous 'Cuninga Street' had for the locals become 'Coney Street' – a place where rabbits or rabbit fur was sold – at least a century before the writers of official documents felt able to accept the change. No one today knows for sure when the people began to talk of 'Coney Street'.

There is another interesting reference by Rebecca to 'Copper gate' and here she seems to envisage an actual large gate, presumably near today's 'Coppergate', a street close to the castle. But as my colleague Magnus Magnusson pointed out, 'Coppergate' does not mean 'gate of copper', it comes from the Scandinavian 'Koppari' and means the street of joiners.

Professor Dobson offered a way out of this apparent contradiction. He assured me that alongside one end of 'Coppergate' would have been one of the large gates leading into the precincts of the castle. And the name 'Coppergate' itself was used in 1190 for this street, since it is mentioned in surviving documents dated sixty years before the massacre.

It was Professor Dobson's knowledge of medieval York that led eventually to the most exciting discovery we made in that city.

The professor took Rebecca's description of how she fled from the castle to a church, and looked for a surviving medieval church that might have been the same one. There were more than forty churches in York at the time of the massacre and about half survive today, in some form or other. But the professor felt that only one – St Mary's, Castlegate – could possibly be the church in which Rebecca hid.

We visited the church in spring 1975, as workmen were beginning to convert the building into a museum. It was as Rebecca described, very close to 'Coppergate' and within sight and earshot of the castle itself. The snag was simply that none of the surviving medieval churches in York has a crypt or cellar, with the single exception of the Cathedral, and Rebecca was specific that she was not hiding there.

From that visit, six months passed and then Professor Dobson wrote to me of a new development at this church, St Mary's, Castlegate:

> In September, during the renovation of the church, a workman certainly found something that seems to have been a crypt – very rare in York except for the Minster – under the chancel of that church. It was blocked up immediately and before the York archaeologists could investigate it properly. But the workman who looked inside said he had seen round stone arches and vaults. Not much to go on, but if he was right this would point to a Norman or Romanesque period of building i.e. before 1190 rather than after it.
>
> So, if one wanted to carry this argument to a conclusion, this crypt could be the place where, if you believe her story, Rebecca met her doom. More certainly still, the discovery of re-used Roman and Anglo-Saxon columns and masonry this summer below the present floor level in St Mary's, makes it absolutely clear there was a church on the site in Rebecca's time.

A chance discovery by a church workman had suddenly made Rebecca's story of murder in a crypt seem much more likely. The entire regression was now a credible account of what might have happened in York in 1190.

Significantly too, her story is not a straightforward re-wording of history-book versions of the massacre. Rebecca knew nothing of the actions taken by the Sheriff and the Constable of the Castle, nor of the promises of safe conduct and the final scenes of murder.

This ignorance is perhaps quite natural if Rebecca is viewed as a genuine eye-witness with an inevitably limited knowledge of events overall during the riots. If we view her regression as a fantasy based on a reading of history books, it is perhaps strange she should have omitted to fantasise about the best known features of most textbook versions of the massacre.

If Rebecca had claimed to have been murdered with the others in the castle, her story would have been historically almost irrefutable. Yet her version was ultimately all the more impressive for being made plausible only by a curious workman's accidental discovery in an ancient church.

Chapter 6

THE ROMAN WIFE

YORK was the setting for another of the seven lives of Jane Evans. Under hypnosis, the twelfth-century Rebecca became Livonia and gave a first-hand account of intrigue and rebellion in Roman Britain about the year AD 286.

This third-century life was the earliest of Jane Evans's six 'previous existences' and it was also the last she recorded for Bloxham. It was after 'Livonia' that she felt so unwell that she refused to do any more. I researched Rebecca and Livonia together simply because I could work on both in the city of York.

Livonia's story is that she is the wife of Titus, a man much older than herself. He is tutor in Latin, Greek and poetry to the son of a prominent Roman named Constantius, whose family live in a villa on the outskirts of Roman York, which Livonia correctly names throughout as 'Eboracum'.

Her narrative, during a tumultuous period of British history, has many more names and facts than the Rebecca regression – as you might expect from an educated woman, closely involved with politics in Roman Britain, compared with the twelfth-century Jewess, who lived within a closed and repressed group in society.

But as the names came tumbling out, and most were historically accurate, there seemed to be an enormous flaw in the narrative. All the history books mention Constantius, the man Livonia unmistakably names as the head of the household, but none place him in Roman Britain in the year AD 286. If Livonia had this central fact wrong, then as far as I could see the entire regression was a fiction.

As it turned out, Livonia knew a great deal more than I

did about what is historically feasible. Strangely, the truth is that history books do not give us Livonia's version of events but they cannot contradict it, because she is talking of 'missing' years in the lives of some of the best known personalities of the Roman world, people whose careers are otherwise well documented.

This entire episode, where Livonia appears to be filling in blank pages in the history books, is so astonishing as to be worth considering in detail. This is how we are introduced to the family in a walled garden of a villa near Eboracum:

Bloxham: Is this your garden?
Livonia: No, it is the garden of the house of the Legate Constantius. His wife. . . .
Bloxham (*interrupting*): What is her name?
Livonia: The Lady Helena.
Bloxham: Is the Lady Helena with you now?
Livonia: We are all in the garden. We are watching the legate's son with his military tutor. They are fighting in the garden. He is teaching him tactics and how to use his sword, his armour and his shield.

Livonia tells us the boy's name is Constantine, and another of his tutors is her husband Titus. But the key point of interest is the father Constantius – just what is he supposed to be doing in Britain in AD 286?

Livonia: When I first came here with my husband, Patronius Aquila was ruling over Britain then. He was in charge and he used to take the waters at Aquae Sulis (the Roman name for the City of Bath, which is famous for its waters) for his aches and pains. He always had aches and pains.
Bloxham: Did he?
Livonia: Yes. He was not a good ruler at all. And then Constantius was put in charge.
Bloxham: Is Constantius a nice man and just?

Livonia: Yes, very just, very good. He has two men under
him, main men under him. One is Caius Flaverius and the
other is Curio, who are in charge of other parts of the
country.

There is no doubt whatever that Livonia is talking about
Aurelius Valerius Constantius, nicknamed 'Chlorus' or 'Pale',
who rose from the ranks of the Roman army to become, eight
years on from this point in Livonia's story, Constantius Caesar,
part-ruler of the Roman empire.

Now the wife of Constantius was certainly named Helena
and their son was indeed Constantine, who many years later
was destined to be known as Constantine the Great, founder
of Constantinople and the Emperor who made Christianity
the official religion of the Roman world.

The problem with this remarkable family was that the
history books do not name Constantius as Governor of Britain
in 286 and do not suggest that he or his family were living at
Eboracum at that time.

Professor Brian Hartley of Leeds University, an authority on
Roman Britain, gave me the answer. He listened to the tape and
agreed it was quite possible for Constantius to have been
governor of Britain, as described by Livonia, because there is
a gap in our knowledge of his career from about AD 283, when
he is known to be governor of Dalmatia, until he re-appears
about 290.

From my own reading, I found too that the governorship of
Britain would have been quite a logical next step for Constantius, governor of Dalmatia, in his progress up the ladder
of Roman politics.

But was he really governor of Britain? I went to the history
books to see if any other Roman is named as governor in this
period. By coincidence there are gaps in our knowledge of
Roman governors, and this is one of them. No one today knows
who was governor in the missing years in the life of Constantius. It could as well have been that gentleman as anybody else.

And there is a third mystery about the family which also dovetails with Livonia's story. The son Constantine had so much written about him, I wondered if his whereabouts in 286 had been recorded. Perhaps his age would discredit the regression by making him too young to be having tuition in weaponry in 286 – perhaps he wasn't even born then?

Not a bit! A great deal is known about the life of Constantine the Great, but his whereabouts in 286 and his date of birth are not included. Even Constantine's official biographer, Eusebius, did not know when the emperor was born.

Guesses about his date of birth have ranged from AD 272 to 280 and Professor Hartley told me historians today favour the earlier date which, as he put it, 'fits Livonia's story rather well'. It would make the boy Constantine fourteen years old when he received his tuition in the use of weapons in that garden in Eboracum.

Interestingly, there is some slight supportive evidence for the family of Constantius being more British than is today supposed – the writings of the twelfth-century monk Geoffrey of Monmouth, whose *History of Britain* is a Latin translation of ancient documents in the old Celtic tongue, which he alleged were found in Brittany. His 'history' was accepted for centuries, but in more recent times was so discredited that he was given the title 'Geoffrey the Liar'.

His work is now generally regarded as a mixture of half-truths, legends and lies, and fortunately his references to the family of Constantius do not remotely resemble Livonia's story – except that he says the wife Helena was a Princess of the British tribe of the Trinovantes, that Constantius married her in this country and that Constantine was conceived in Britain. Other documents from the thirteenth century in the town of Colchester repeat the story that Helena was a local woman, although modern history books assert, without much conviction, that Helena was probably the daughter of a central European innkeeper.

But modern researches have found some bases of truth in Geoffrey's garbled histories, and perhaps the idea, shared with

Livonia, that Constantius might have spent some of the lost years in Britain, is one of them.

Nor can the regression be dismissed as a fiction built around a blank area of history. Livonia knows a considerable number of verifiable historical facts that fit perfectly into her version of the missing years. No modern student of history could contradict the names and events she describes, as she tells of preparations for a banquet in Constantius's villa, listing 'meat and fowl, fruit and Cyprus wines in silver goblets'. It is a farewell occasion, but treachery and rebellion are in the offing.

Livonia: A messenger has come from Rome for Constantius. He has called Titus and me and the domina (Latin:'lady of the house') already knows the news that a man called Allectus has come with a message for Constantius. He has been summoned back to Rome. Rome now has two emperors – two emperors.

Bloxham: Who are they?

Livonia: The Emperor Diocletian and the Emperor Maximianus. There are now two emperors of Rome.

Bloxham: How will this affect you?

Livonia: Not at all, except that the legate has to go to Rome to Maximianus who is now in charge of Britain, who now governs Britain. The empire has been split in two – Diocletian has one half and Maximianus the half which includes Britain.

Indeed they had! Diocletian had become emperor in 284, but felt he wanted to share power with someone he trusted, so in 286 he appointed Maximianus, a peasant's son from Illyria, his co-ruler and gave him the western half of the empire.

It was interesting too to observe how Bloxham's subjects never get ahead of themselves when talking about their previous 'lives'. At any given moment, they may talk about their pasts, but the next step in their story is as unknown as next year is to us. A person re-telling a story from history has knowledge of the outcome at every stage; not so with Livonia, who is clearly re-living her experiences and seems unaware of events she will herself describe a few minutes later.

For instance, asked how the recall of Constantius and the division of the empire will affect the family, Livonia says 'not at all'. As her own narrative unfolds it will be seen the effect is shattering upon the lives of every person who was in the garden – the family are never to be united again.

Yet if Livonia felt a false sense of security at this stage, she nevertheless had an entirely correct feminine intuition about Allectus, the man who brought the news of Constantius's return to Rome.

> Livonia: I do not like this man Allectus. My husband says it's a woman's fancy, but I do not like him.
> Bloxham: Do you like living here?
> Livonia: Yes, we are very happy. But we are worried about Constantius going back. I don't like this man Allectus, he has cold eyes – cold eyes.
> Bloxham: And he is going to be the new ruler?
> Livonia: No. Constantius, so my husband tells me, has to put men in charge in his place when he goes to Rome. My husband thinks he is making Valerius or Curio responsible for the south and the other for the north. But he is leaving these two men in charge when he leaves.
> Bloxham: What do you think will happen to Constantius when he gets back to Rome?
> Livonia: We do not know why he has been summoned. We think it might be that now Maximianus is emperor with Diocletian, he wants to see all the men who are in charge of the various parts of the empire. But I don't like this man Allectus. I don't like his manner at all.
> Bloxham: When did you first meet him?
> Livonia: He came to the house today, but I don't like him.
> Bloxham: Is that the first time you have ever seen him?
> Livonia: Yes – he has very cold eyes – cold eyes.
> Bloxham: Had he his wife with him?

Livonia: No. He had come from Rome, but it is strange –
Titus was telling me he had come from Rome with an
urgent message for Constantius, and yet he stopped at
Gessoriacum (Roman name for the French port of
Boulogne) – to see Carausius, who is in charge of the
fleet. And why should he stop if it was so important he
should get to Constantius quickly – I don't like Allectus –
– I don't like Allectus.

History may be vague about the whereabouts of Constantius
and his family in this fateful year 286, but there is no doubt
Allectus was in Britain and scheming to secure power. Allectus,
along with the Roman Admiral Carausius, who was in charge
of a fleet at Gessoriacum (Boulogne), plotted to overthrow
Roman rule in Britain. Because they succeeded for some years,
the faces of the conspirators can be seen today on coins issued
for the independent Britain.

Livonia gives a basically accurate picture of this quite
obscure historical event, the revolt against Roman rule of
AD 286.

Bloxham: Now this is a little later. What is happening now?
Livonia: We are on our way to Verulam (Verulamium was
the Roman name for the city of St Albans). The domina,
Constantine, Favonius, Hilary and me and Titus. We are
on our way – it's dark. (*Pause.*) I knew we shouldn't trust
Allectus – when Constantius had sailed for Rome, Carausius brought the fleet over. He landed and he has conquered Britain – Carausius has come over and he has
taken over and we have had to flee – Allectus came to
our house – killed some of our servants – but Favonius
managed to kill some of Allectus's men and we have had
to go by dark.
We are going to Verulam and the small villa that we saw.
It was terrible – they killed some of the servants and
domina Helena said we had to escape and we had to pack
up quickly and we are going by night and resting by day

– but we are going by night to Verulam because nobody knows us there – because if they knew that Constantius's wife and son Constantine are in Verulam, they will come for us – we are going to the small villa in Verulam – Allectus, I didn't like Allectus.

Bloxham: You judged him right didn't you?

Livonia: And now Carausius rules Britain – Carausius rules Britain.

Bloxham: Is he a bad man?

Livonia: Yes – Carausius rules Britain – he was in charge of the fleet, the Roman fleet at Gessoriacum and he has brought the fleet over here now and he has taken over Britain – it no longer belongs to Rome – it belongs to Carausius.

Bloxham: Oh I see. It belongs to Carausius not to Rome?

Livonia: He has conquered Britain. He conquered Londinium and he is coming up to Eboracum and we have had to flee by the backroads and the sideroads and fields to Verulam. (*Pause.*) Valerius is dead.

Bloxham: He is dead?

Livonia: Valerius is dead – Curio is still alive, but Valerius is dead – we are going to Verulam.

Valerius and Curio, the two men Livonia claims were left in charge of Britain, are untraceable. Little is known today of the insurrection, but Marcus Aurelius Carausius was proclaimed emperor of an independent Britain in AD 287 and Allectus was at his side as chancellor.

Before leading his rebellion, this Roman Admiral had also been summoned back to Rome by the new joint emperors, and conceivably Allectus had brought him this news. However, the history books say that Carausius feared he would be put on trial if he went to Rome. It was said that he and his fleet used to wait until pirates had sacked a town or ship before intercepting them – a working method which meant that Roman justice sometimes got its pirates, and Carausius usually got the booty. Bribery was another of his weaknesses, but he was a natural fighting man and, rather than risk trial, he saw in the confusion of a newly divided empire a chance for conquest.

Between them, Carausius and Allectus held Britain independent of Rome for nine years, before it was re-conquered by none other than Constantius himself!

Livonia and Helena spent the years quietly in hiding, but the narrative returns to known historical facts with the final overthrow of Carausius and Allectus.

Bloxham: Have you heard any more about Allectus?

Livonia: Allectus murdered Carausius.

Bloxham (*clearly startled*): What?

Livonia: Allectus murdered Carausius and when he murdered Carausius news came that Rome had declared war on Britain. And Allectus had just murdered Carausius and Allectus is now at war with Rome.

Bloxham: Are they sending men over?

Livonia: Yes. Yes. We think that Constantius will be coming back.

And so he was, for in 293 Constantius and the Roman legions had captured Gessoriacum, Carausius's naval base in France. Allectus, the chancellor, then murdered Carausius, declared himself Emperor of Britain and waited to repel the invading legions of Rome. The invasion came in 296 and, as Livonia later says, Allectus was killed and Roman rule re-established by Constantius.

According to Livonia, Helena and her household returned to Eboracum to wait for Constantius, but there was an unpleasant surprise in store for them.

Livonia: When we got to Eboracum we found that all sorts of things had arrived before us from Constantius. So the domina is right. He is coming back. He has sent on beautiful carpets, beautiful material, and she is very excited but very distressed in a way because Allectus had lived at the villa for a time and the garden is terrible. But that can wait. She is busy now making us all run around and tidy things up. We are just waiting for Constantius to return. It has been a long time.

Bloxham: What has happened to Allectus?

Livonia: Allectus is dead.

Bloxham: Did someone kill him?

Livonia: I think so. We haven't heard very much because we've been rushing here to get ready for the return of Constantius. And we are waiting for him to arrive. And Curio has arrived. Curio has arrived and he looks terrible. He has called my husband aside and he is telling him something. Favonius is with them – and Curio is going. (*Pause.*) Titus is coming to tell me. Oh, poor domina, oh! She is waiting for Constantius, but she does not know that Curio is going to tell her that Constantius has rejected her and has married the daughter of Maximianus – Theodora – and he is bringing her here. He is bringing the Princess Theodora here and yet the domina is waiting for him here – what can we do?

Bloxham: I thought they were happy together?

Livonia: Yes. There must be a reason. Curio told Titus that they have made Constantius – Caesar Constantius. And they have made a man called Galerius – Caesar Galerius. And Constantius married Theodora the daughter of Maximianus, and Galerius married the daughter of Diocletian. (*Pause.*) And Titus tells me he (Constantius) had to renounce his first wife in the Temple of Jupiter and take the Princess Theodora as his wife. He already has a child – two children – by her.

A complicated piece of matchmaking, but all perfectly true. The joint emperors, for reasons of state, married their daughters to strong and powerful Romans, who were created minor Caesars. So Constantius was persuaded to renounce Helena and marry the Princess Theodora, and the other chosen bridegroom was Galerius who married Valeria, the daughter of Diocletian.

Livonia mentions also that Constantius and Theodora soon had two children. By the time Constantius died in Eboracum in 306, ten years after defeating Allectus, the couple had six children – three boys and three girls. But on the death of Constantius Caesar, it was Constantine, his son by the rejected Helena, who was acclaimed Caesar by the legions in Britain and who went on to become sole ruler of the empire.

Poor Livonia knew nothing of the great future awaiting her husband's pupil, for she says that she and Titus were both killed during the reign of the Emperor Diocletian, which ended in 305, earlier than the death of Constantius.

The manner of her death is again violent, and the circumstances as fascinating as anything that had gone before. She says that Helena, learning she was divorced by her husband, retraced her steps to Verulamium. Here she became interested in Christianity, being introduced by Titus to a prominent Christian of the area, a woodcarver named Albanus.

Now Livonia had mentioned earlier, during the family's first long stay in Verulamium, how Titus and she were converted to Christianity by this woodcarver. On the family's return, Albanus was introduced to both Helena and the son Constantine.

Titus was the most fervent convert and Livonia became anxious, because 'Galerius has passed an edict about Christians that they should all be killed'. It is a fact that Diocletian, Galerius's sponsor, sanctioned such a proclamation and initiated the last great Roman purge of Christians, and Livonia was entitled to be fearful, especially since her husband was contemplating an extreme step.

Livonia: . . . and I am worried now because Titus is going to be a priest. They are only waiting for a man to come to make him a priest. They are all anxiously awaiting this man and when he comes Titus will be made a priest.
Bloxham: Do you know the name of the man who is being sent to make him a priest?
Livonia: I think it is Ossius.

C

Bloxham: Where does Ossius come from?

Livonia: I don't know. They are waiting for him to come. He has been going around all the Christian places to see the people who are Christians. He is from – I think he is from – oh I cannot remember the place. He is not from Britain.

Bloxham: Not from Britain?

Livonia: We are going to the house of a man in Verulam. I said I'd go because Titus is going to be made a priest. But we are waiting for Ossius to come.

Bloxham: Now it is a little bit later. Is Ossius here yet?

Livonia: Yes, we are going to Verulam to the house. We are on our way, but I am nervous because of all the awful things that have been happening. They are burning the houses of Christians in other towns. We are going to the house because Titus is going to be made a priest.

Bloxham: Now you are at the house – is it the house of Albanus?

Livonia: No, it is the house of somebody else. I don't know the name. We don't know the names of these people very much, but it is dark in the room and there are candles and I am nervous. Titus is not with me, he has gone with Albanus and I am frightened. I am frightened. It is too quiet, but they say there is nothing to be frightened about because their God will look after me.

Bloxham: You are going to be all right? You were not there when he was going to be made a priest were you?

Livonia: No, I was frightened. I came home. I came out. I came out and I came home. I am waiting for Titus to come home, but he does not come. Titus does not come. Favonius. . . .

Bloxham: What about Favonius?

Livonia: He has come to tell me that Titus is dead.

Bloxham: Titus is dead?

Livonia: They burned the house. Why? Why? They are not doing any harm. Titus is dead, Albanus escaped. Titus is dead.

Bloxham: Who do you think gave them away?

Livonia: I don't know. (*Pause.*) Titus is dead. I am going out to see if I can see where they are. I am going to see if I can find Titus. Favonius is coming with me. (*Pause.*) We are trying to find the house. (*Terror in voice.*) It is all in flames. It is all flames around us. The soldiers are coming, soldiers are coming down the streets. They stopped, stopping us? (*Pause.*) No, Favonius says we are not Christians. Favonius and I walk on – they know Favonius – we are trying to find – I do not remember where the house is where I left Titus – and I came out because I was frightened. There are houses in flames all about. I should have stayed with him – I should have stayed with him.

I am going along and there are a lot of people rushing around – and (*panic*) where is Favonius? He is gone – Favonius has gone – I am on my own and people are running – people are running – soldiers are coming – everyone is running and I can't find Favonius – he is big – I must find Favonius – and I can't find the house where I left Titus and people are running all around me and they are all screaming and shouting – the flames and the soldiers are coming down – Oh no, no don't.

At this point, Livonia in some terror apparently died. The end, in flames and violence, is similar to her death as the Jewess Rebecca, although such scenes are not repeated in any of her other four regressions.

Livonia died during a phase of the persecution of Christians by the Emperor Diocletian, when churches and meeting places were burned and Christians slaughtered, despite the efforts of Constantius Caesar to minimise the bloodshed in Britain.

What is not clear is whether Livonia's Christian woodcarver Albanus is meant to be the man we know today as Saint Alban, from whom present day Verulamium takes its name of St Albans. Little is known of St Alban, except that he was a Christian martyr in Verulamium, and his death has often been attributed to the persecutions of Diocletian.

Whether this man is St Alban or not, the idea that the family and servants of Helena might have been strongly influenced at this time by a Christian sect has credibility. For another of the mysteries surrounding this family is the source of the faith which converted Helena and her son Constantine into two of the best known Christians of all time.

In later life, Helena showed such Christian zeal that she was eventually canonised as St Helena. And Constantine the Great was of course the emperor who deposed the pagan gods of Rome and established Christian worship in their place.

From his earliest battles, soon after the death of his father at Eboracum, Constantine the Great fought with a Christian monogram painted on the shield of every soldier. This device, a cross made from a spear and carrying the first two letters of Christ, Constantine later incorporated into the imperial Roman standard or labarum.

According to the ancient writer Lactantius, Constantine was instructed in a dream to adopt this Christian emblem. Eusebius on the other hand claimed Constantine was converted when he looked at the sky and saw a vision of a cross set against the sun, with the words 'in this sign I conquer'.

But more modern writers have pointed out that Constantine's faith was too profound to be caused simply by a mystical sign that appeared to bring success in battle. They have suggested that Constantine's faith was based upon the influence of a Spanish Bishop, who was the emperor's chief religious adviser.

This man was Bishop Hosius or Ossius of Cordoba, and he seems to be a direct link with Livonia's story, for it was Ossius 'not from Britain' who came to Verulam to ordain her husband as a priest on the night of Livonia's death.

Could Christianity have conceivably begun to grip Constantine on that very night? Might not Ossius have sought sanctuary from the soldiers quite naturally in the house of Helena, and there possibly have begun a lasting relationship with the family?

If some historians already believe Hosius was the person

who converted Constantine to the new faith, might it not have happened in Britain as a logical sequel to the events Livonia has described? In the year AD 324 Constantine the Great wrote that he had come 'from the farthest shores of Britain as God's chosen instrument', so perhaps Britain is the key to much more of the truth about this remarkable Roman family than is currently accepted.

A few days after listening to the Livonia tape and studying a transcript, Professor Brian Hartley gave his verdict on the general historical context of the Livonia regression: 'on the whole it is fairly convincing and checks out, as far as one can check, against known historical facts.'

Some details the professor was not happy about. Describing the villa, Livonia made no reference to any bath house on the heated Turkish bath principle, but spoke of a central pool, which sounded rather like a villa design from an earlier period in the empire. And mention of Roman ladies riding on horseback, and not in light carriages, the professor found jarring. He would have also expected more references to Romans by their full three names.

Both Professor Hartley and Magnus Magnusson noticed too that one Roman fully named by Livonia – the military tutor Marcus Favonius Facilis – bore the same name as a centurion whose tombstone survives today in the Colchester and Essex Museum. But the dates did not appear to fit! So is Livonia's 'Favonius' a later centurion with the same name as the Roman buried at Colchester – is the dating of that tombstone accurate beyond all doubt? Could they be the same man?

The Colchester centurion is thought to have lived two hundred years before the insurrection by Allectus, but there is no date on the tombstone, which is believed to be from the first century because of the style of some white pottery found in the grave area and the clear lettering on the inscription.

Oddly enough there is another link between the town of Colchester and the family of Constantius. The patron saint of the town is Helena, which may be simply a consequence of that unreliable historian Geoffrey of Monmouth's claim that she was a local woman; but if Helena was born in Colchester, it would be virtually certain that any centurion in her employ would have visited the town and might well be buried here.

Aside from such speculation, Professor Hartley told me that Livonia 'knew some quite remarkable historical facts, and numerous published works would have to be consulted if anyone tried to prepare the outline of such a story.'

Professor Hartley's final inscrutable comment was: 'If the lady is hypnotised again, please ask where the amphitheatre was – we've never been able to find it!'

Chapter 7

A SERVANT IN MEDIEVAL FRANCE

THE ancient city of Bourges in the Loire Valley of France was a location for one of the regressions of Jane Evans. Here I visited a mansion where Jane appeared to have lived in the fifteenth century. In this superb house, now preserved as a museum, I was a tourist with a difference – my guide was the tape-recorded voice of a woman who has never seen Bourges, yet who could describe with some accuracy the courtyard, the house, its style of architecture, even the paintings and the people who had filled the long galleries and ornate rooms in the year 1450.

It was an odd experience, since Jane Evans has never been to the Loire Valley, just as she says she had never heard of the house at Bourges, which once belonged to a French merchant prince, Jacques Coeur. Jane Evans is no student of French history, and in any case some of the details of her account of Coeur and his possessions do not seem ever to have been published in English.

In this regression, Jane becomes Alison, teenage servant to Jacques Coeur, an exceptionally wealthy merchant, financier and adviser to King Charles VII. At his peak Coeur was the second most powerful man in France, and his downfall was suitably dramatic. He was falsely accused of poisoning the king's mistress and Alison reopens this five hundred years old murder mystery. Coeur's real mistake was that he loaned huge sums of money to the king and other nobles. He was tried for his life on trumped-up charges, but the significant part of his sentence declared that his wealth was confiscated by the crown and debts owed to Coeur were cancelled.

Alison's complex story of Coeur's wealth, his intrigues with court personalities, his love for the king's mistress, Agnes Sorel, was at first difficult to verify even in outline. Books about Coeur in English are not easily obtained and in frustration I flew to Paris. In the library of Sainte Geneviève, with an able interpreter, I spent hours studying French histories before concluding that Jane Evans, a Welsh housewife, knew a remarkable amount about medieval French history.

In the English language, I have not been able to identify many possible sources for her knowledge of this man. The *Encyclopaedia Britannica* lists only one work in English about him – A. B. Kerr's *Jacques Coeur, Merchant Prince of the Middle Ages* published in 1927. And Kerr himself says in his preface that there had been only one previous biography, by Louisa Stuart Costello back in 1847.

Librarians can offer only these two old books about Jacques Coeur, and having read both, it is clear to me that Alison's familiarity with certain aspects of Coeur's life must come from sources other than these. Some of Alison's assertions I was able to confirm only on the spot in France in conversation with French historians. The odd thing is that even amongst the French, Coeur is not a particularly well known historical personality. Jean Favière in a booklet about him says : 'Who then was this man to whom the history books devote only one or two lines?'

Alison knows a great deal about this man and, like the other regressions, her story is no dry recitation of historical facts. Until Coeur's arrest, which triggers off her own suicide, we have the highly personalised view of a rather reserved and innocent young woman existing on the outer fringes of court life. The servant, possibly eventually the mistress, of a powerful man in court politics, Alison passes on gossip about court life – information she seems mainly to get from Coeur himself.

Historians verified much of what she said; against some of the rest they said 'possibly but we cannot say for certain'. And before we left France, we made one discovery about 'a golden apple of Jacques Coeur' as exciting as the find of a crypt in that church in York which bolstered the Rebecca regression.

Alison's is the story of a young girl who can gradually be seen, although she will not acknowledge it, to be falling in love with Coeur – an affection which ends with her suicide. Her story also has one serious, and possibly very human, blemish. This young girl who knows so much fine detail about Coeur's life and affairs, does not know, or cannot bring herself to admit, that Jacques Coeur is married!

Under hypnosis, Alison begins by seeing colours which suddenly become clear – they are 'rolls of cloth, red, gold green'. These belong to her master, Jacques Coeur, and although there are few surviving portraits of him, her description is true to life.

Bloxham: What is he like?

Alison: Medium height – black tunic edged in miniver – red hose.

Bloxham: What is your master's face like?

Alison: Thin – thin face – clever face.

Bloxham: Has he a big nose?

Alison: No, no! (*Pause.*) Medium height – all those lovely clothes, very beautifully dressed as one who is rich can dress, simply but beautifully – he is wearing a black velvet tunic edged with fur – red hose, fine silk hose, beautiful shoes of red – he said they were Cordovan leather – and he has a jewelled belt around his waist and a chain around his neck.

It is not simply Alison's evident admiration for Coeur which shines through, for in real life the man was famed for his elegance. He dressed as well as the King. Later, when on trial for his life, the question was raised about how Coeur usually dressed. A servant, André Vidal, gave evidence and described a colour scheme remarkably like Alison's version. He had frequently seen his master wearing garments coloured red and black and wearing a gold chain about his neck.

Alison's description 'edged in miniver' comes from the original French *Minu ver* or 'little fur' and is lambskin dotted with ermine. Her often very detailed descriptions of clothes are generally true to the fashions of the fifteenth century.

Bloxham continued to ask what people were wearing and was told that one of the servants was dressed 'differently to the others'. Alison said this was 'Abdul, who is the master's servant'. Later in the regression she referred to Abdul as Coeur's 'body servant'.

In the records of Coeur's trial is testimony that Coeur had 'an Egyptian body slave' – but in the summaries of the trial I read, there was no name for this Egyptian.

Bloxham next moved the questioning to Alison's own background.

Bloxham: And what is your name?
Alison: I am called Alison.
Bloxham: And who are you?
Alison: The master brought me from Alexandria.
Bloxham: Are you happy?
Alison: Oh yes. He is very good. He has called me – he bought me as a young girl and brought me back to his home and taught me to read and write – and called me Alison.
Bloxham: What was your name previously?
Alison: I don't know. I had no name.
Bloxham: Are you pretty?
Alison: No, no. My dresses are nice. My master brings materials from all over, all over, and sells them.
Bloxham: Where did your master buy you? Was it in the market?
Alison: No, no. He was – I was ill and he saw me – he came to the house of my master in Alexandria – I was only young and I was ill and nobody wanted me – and he brought me back and has been very kind to me.

Jacques Coeur had much to do with Alexandria. He built

up a huge trade with the ports of Alexandria, Beirut and Cairo, and both Coeur and his ships were well known throughout the Arab world, where he had been given special permission by the Pope to 'trade with the infidel'. This licence made Coeur's fortune, for he traded not only for Eastern cloths, jewels and spices, but also exchanged French silver for Arab gold by the boatload. It is recorded that every cargo of silver was matched by a tonnage of gold which immediately doubled Coeur's capital investment. The French soon had a saying – 'as rich as Jacques Coeur'.

As for Alison, a name entirely apt for France during that century, there is no record of her in the history books. This is hardly surprising since Coeur at the peak of his wealth had more than forty great mansions and estates in France, all doubtless filled with servants.

But basically, Coeur lived at Bourges, his home town, where he owned several houses and built his beautiful mansion *'La Chaussée'*. Alison relates that Coeur owned 'many houses' but says he lived at Bourges and 'goes to all the fairs at Lyons to sell his materials'.

This too is certainly true, for Coeur is celebrated as the man who revived the ancient Lyons fairs.

Alison then tells Bloxham that a visitor is expected at Coeur's house.

Alison: She – we are still waiting for her, there is great excitement, great excitement – she is said to be very beautiful.
Bloxham: Can you tell me her name?
Alison: Men call her the Maid from Fromenteau.
Bloxham: Is she a very special person?
Alison: Oh yes.
Bloxham: In what way is she special?
Alison: She is the mistress of the King.
Bloxham: Oh, which King?
Alison: Charles. (*Pause – then hesitantly mutters a name.*)
Bloxham: Francois?

Alison: No, no. (*Pause.*) I can't remember. (*Pause.*) Charles
– Charles de Valois!

Bloxham: What does your master think of the King as a
man?

Alison: Not very much. (*Pause.*) He is very fond of Agnes
Sorel, the Maid of Fromenteau.

Bloxham: Agnes what?

Alison: Sorel – the Maid of Fromenteau.

The references are accurate. Charles VII had the family
name of Valois. The mistress of Charles de Valois was Agnes
Sorel, celebrated for her beauty and born in 1422 in the small
town of Fromenteau in Touraine. She dominated the king's life
for five years until her sudden death in 1449. It was generally
accepted that the king thought more of Agnes than he did of
his queen. Since Agnes is thought to have become the king's
mistress in 1444, this presumably is the year Alison is describing.

Bloxham: Now this is a bit later. This lady has arrived –
are you attracted to her?

Alison: She is beautiful, beautiful – beautiful clothes.

Bloxham: What is she wearing?

Alison: A dress of green brocade, with half moons and stars
embroidered, and velvet cloak edged with fur – and a
hood. But she is beautiful. (*Pause.*) They say she is come
to borrow money from the master for the king.

Bloxham: And is your master going to lend money for the
king?

Alison: Yes, yes. He has lent money to the king before.

Bloxham: Is your master titled?

Alison: Just Jacques Coeur, merchant prince.

Bloxham: How much money did he lend the king?

Alison: Two thousand écus d'or, which has been wasted.

It was some time before I realised Alison was saying '*écus
d'or*' meaning 'golden *écus*'. An *écu* was a coin, now obsolete,

which had been introduced in France in 1395. It was the main coinage in the days of Charles VII.

Bloxham: How did he waste it?
Alison: He borrowed it for his armies, but he built a new tower against the castle instead. (*Pause.*) The Maid of Fromenteau has come instead of the king to borrow money.

French historians smiled when they heard that Charles VII was supposed to have spent the wages of his armies on building an extension to a castle – and then sent along his mistress to borrow more money. They said it sounded fairly consistent behaviour for Charles de Valois!

A visit by Agnes Sorel to Coeur also sounded likely since there was a close relationship between them. It was rumoured that they were lovers, but certainly she was a close friend and ally of Coeur at court, and on her death he was named as executor in her will.

Bloxham: What did she say to your master? You can hear the conversation?
Alison: He showed her all the beautiful cloths. He admires her – she is very beautiful and she wants the money for the King. He said he would not lend it for the King but he would lend it for her. And in return she would wear his silks and jewels so that people would know that Jacques Coeur could get these materials and would come to him for them – and that would be his surety.

The court of Charles VII did indeed wear the clothes and jewels provided by Jacques Coeur. Could this transaction have been the origin of the custom?

Bloxham: Did she speak to you?
Alison: No. She is very beautiful. She is called Agnes.
Bloxham: Did he introduce you?

Alison: No. (*Pause.*) But he gave her a diamond. He said it was the first polished diamond in France. (*Pause.*) She wanted rubies but he said only diamonds would suit her – and he gave her a diamond with a sapphire clasp at the back.

Some historians have said that Coeur was the first man to have diamonds shaped and cut, and also that Agnes Sorel was the first person in France to wear them. One French historian wrote: 'Agnes introduced the wearing of pearls and faceted diamonds from the fabulous storehouse of her friend Jacques Coeur.'

Bloxham: Was the diamond as big as your little finger nail?
Alison: Much bigger and the chain and sapphire clasp. She did not want to take it, but he said she was to take it. My master admires beauty. He has no interest in women except for their beauty.
Bloxham: I expect he admires you doesn't he?
Alison: He is fond of me. He has taught me to read and to write.
Bloxham: Are you fond of him?
Alison: Yes, he has been very kind to me.
Bloxham: Are you married to him?
Alison: No, no.
Bloxham: Are you his mistress?
Alison: No.
Bloxham: What is happening now?
Alison: The master has gone to the castle.
Bloxham: The castle where the King is?
Alison: Yes, at Chinon.
Bloxham: At Chinon?
Alison: At Chinon, the castle at Chinon – the castle is called Mehun-sur-Yèvre.

Here Alison is confused about the names of two castles in the Loire Valley, which she has telescoped into one. The King's favourite castle was at Mehun-sur-Yèvre, quite close to Bourges, whilst Chinon is another castle, some miles away, where the King also lived for long periods. Since Alison, a servant, is unlikely to have visited either castle, perhaps it is excusable that she should imagine they are the same place.

Alison : . . . he is going to see the Duchess Yolande.
Bloxham : The Duchess Yolande ?
Alison : The Duchess Yolande who is Charles de Valois' mother. He told me he thinks they are going to try to borrow more money from him for the armies.

The King borrowed money from Coeur on numerous occasions, usually never to be repaid. Some of the unpaid receipts survive to this day. An interesting minor 'inaccuracy' is the reference to Yolande as Charles' 'mother' – a false assumption that one would not get from a history book but which might be a quite natural mistake for a girl in Alison's position. Yolande, Duchess of Anjou, was not the King's mother but a rather special mother-in-law, for Charles had been engaged to be married from the age of thirteen and Yolande virtually raised him. She was certainly a mother figure to the King.

Bloxham : Has he (Coeur) taken you to Persia or any of these places ?
Alison : No. He doesn't go much himself now. He is known, his name is as familiar in Persia and the far countries as it is in France. They all know and respect the name of Jacques Coeur. Some say he is Jewish, but he is a Frenchman born in Bourges – his father was a goldsmith.

Historians in France told me there was speculation in the fifteenth century that perhaps Coeur was Jewish. There are two stories of his origins – one that he was the son of a Bourges dealer in furs and skins, and another that his father was a Bourges goldsmith. The goldsmith version seems plausible because Coeur undoubtedly had a great knowledge of precious metals and stones and as quite a young man knew enough to become head of the mint at Bourges.

Bloxham: Are you in love with anyone?
Alison: No.
Bloxham (*sensing some uncertainty*): Aren't you?
Alison: No.
Bloxham: Have you had any special people come to see you lately? Or to see your master?
Alison: The Duchess Yolande has been several times.
Bloxham: Has she? Is she a nice woman?
Alison: She is said to possess the brain of a man. She is the most cunning woman in all France.

A deserved reputation for Yolande of Aragon, Duchess of Anjou, who was feared and respected. She had single-handedly administered Anjou, had successfully fought off English attempts to annex it, and was not above murder as a political weapon.

Bloxham: What did she say to you?
Alison: I am just Alison who writes for my master and looks after him. She – I am nothing for the likes of the Duchess Yolande.
Bloxham: But I expect she has spoken to you hasn't she?
Alison: Yes.
Bloxham: What did she say to you?
Alison: Just pleasantries.
Bloxham: Did the Duchess Yolande borrow money?
Alison: For the King, yes. (*Pause.*) They call him heron legs.
Bloxham: Heron legs?
Alison: Heron legs, he has thin spindly legs, with a Valois nose – a long Valois nose – spindly heron legs.

Indeed he had. His nose looms large even from the royal portraits that survive today. And French historians assure me that he looked such a ridiculous figure in yellow tights that he was mockingly referred to in fifteenth-century France as 'heron legs'.

Bloxham: That's Charles?
Alison: That is Charles de Valois. But he is doing nothing to save France. (*Pause.*) People say it was he who had the Maid of Orleans handed over to the English.

One of the great historical controversies is whether Charles VII might have betrayed Joan of Arc to the English. She was burned at the stake in 1431, while Jacques Coeur was still an ambitious young merchant.

The King made no effort to save or ransom her, and popular opinion blamed him for her death.

But Bloxham returns to the intriguing question of the relationship between Alison and Coeur, a man much older than the girl he took as a servant, although he now clearly has a special regard for her. In this passage Alison makes what is arguably the first major blunder of any of the regressions so far.

Alison: He is very kind to me, I have a beautiful room of my own. I am like his daughter, beautiful clothes. He confides in me, he talks to me. I have lovely porcelain that he has given me and I have it in my room – and jewellery. And he likes me to dress well. He is there when the seamstress comes and tells her what he would like.
Bloxham: What is your favourite dress?
Alison: One of pale green brocade with a low bodice and open sleeves, sleeves slashed from the top of the arm to the wrist, so that the arms can be seen.
Bloxham: Do you wear any jewels?
Alison (*sadly*): I don't go anywhere to wear any jewels.
Bloxham: Don't you like wearing them at home?
Alison: Yes, but there is nobody there to see them.
Bloxham: Has your master ever been married?

Alison: No, not that I know of. He loves only beautiful
things. He has no love for men or women, only beautiful
people, beautiful things. He admires me for my – well my
good looks but does not desire me.

The significant question is whether Jacques Coeur has ever
been married and the response 'no, not that I know of'. The
fact is Jacques Coeur was a married man and by this stage of
his life had five virtually grown up children – one of whom
was about to become a bishop, thanks to Coeur's influence!
Many years before, as an ambitious young man, Jacques had
married Macée de Leodepart, daughter of a wealthy Bourges
family.

How is it that this girl can know Coeur had an Egyptian
body slave, and not be aware that he was married with five
children – a fact published in every historical account of
Coeur's life?

Of course, there is nothing in the history books to tell us
whether Coeur and his wife were happily married at this time.
There have always been rumours about his relationship with
Agnes Sorel, the King's mistress. Arguably, if he was no longer
actively or happily married, in days before divorce, he had
little problem about leading a double life, since he had over
forty households, including several in Bourges, and could
conveniently see as much or as little of his wife as he
pleased.

But would a trusted servant such as Alison have been in
ignorance of the existence of a wife? Coeur was a secretive
and close-mouthed man certainly, as some of the mysterious
mottoes he had carved in stone in his new house at Bourges
indicate: 'say, do, keep silent of my joy (or love)', is just one.
But Alison would surely have been told by other servants that
her master was married, even if at this stage in the regression
she had never lived under the same roof as Macée de Leodepart?

The reader will have to form his or her own judgement.
Some BBC colleagues, who have heard the tape, regard it as a

cardinal error, others are prepared to see it as a simple lapse of memory by the hypnotised Jane Evans, who, after all, is casting her mind back five hundred years!

Some have seen it as a human failing on the part of a teenage girl, infatuated by Coeur, who even today cannot face the full reality of all his circumstances – namely that he was a married man.

Oddly, if the explanation for the entire regression is a reading of history books in the twentieth century, then I cannot explain how Bloxham's subject would not know of the marriage. It is one of the most prominent features in every account I have read.

Alison next makes a passing reference to Jacques Coeur's appointment as '*argentier* to the King', or King's Treasurer, in 1439. She also mentions the King sending money 'for the release of his brother Réné d'Anjou who has been held prisoner'. Again history is on her side, for Réné d'Anjou was the King's brother by marriage, the son of Yolande, and was a prisoner of the Duke of Burgundy for five years before being ransomed.

Bloxham: Did he (Coeur) tell you anything else?
Alison: He told me that the King had banished the Dauphin. Louis had been banished from the Court – he was rude to Agnes Sorel and he was banished from the court; and my master fears that he may take revenge on Agnes – my master feels he will.
Bloxham: In what way was he rude to her?
Alison: He insulted her, tried to make advances to her, and the King was very angry and so was the fair Agnes. And he has banished him from the Court.

The dauphin or heir to the throne, later King Louis XI, was banished from court and there was much animosity between Louis and both his father and his father's mistress. Louis once slapped Agnes Sorel's face in public and chased her round the court with a sword. But Alison hints at darker secrets in the life of Louis, this future king of France.

Alison: And it is whispered that Louis killed his wife, Margaret of Scotland, who came here – the dauphine was very sweet, my master tells me she was very sweet – and he – she died and my master thinks it was Louis who was responsible.

A succinct version of the gossip of the time. Margaret of Scotland, young wife of Louis and daughter of King James I of Scotland, died mysteriously in 1446. Her 'gentleness and love of poetry' made her a favourite of King Charles who had arranged her marriage to strengthen his alliance with Scotland – he had hoped for Scottish soldiers in his earlier fight for his crown. But Margaret was a sad figure, openly despised by her husband.

Incredibly, they were engaged when Margaret was three years old and Louis was five. They were married when he was thirteen and she was eleven! At the age of twenty, Margaret of Scotland was suddenly taken ill at a banquet and died. There were rumours that Louis had poisoned her.

Later in his life, Louis was referred to as the '*universelle aragne*' or universal spider. He was hated and feared and one historian, Professor François Marie-Joseph Crouzet of the University of Bordeaux, said his character consisted of 'piety combined with ruthlessness'. Compare that verdict with Alison's assessment:

Alison: . . . Louis is very wicked, very cruel and yet he is pious sometimes.
Bloxham: That's rather a contradiction isn't it?
Alison: Yes. He kills someone one day and begs the Blessed Virgin for forgiveness the next. The fair Agnes laughs at him. Yes, my master says the fair Agnes laughs at him.

The constantly used phrase 'the fair Agnes' is clearly a translation of 'la belle Agnes', as she was often referred to in the fifteenth century.

Bloxham: This is a little later. What are you doing now?

Alison: I am still in the house at Bourges, but my master has ridden to Chinon – to get the ladies ready, for Charles de Valois is going to Paris again. He's going to Paris – he was angry with the people of Paris and did not go to Paris for many years. But he is going to Paris and my master has gone to take clothes for the ladies to wear for their entry into Paris.

When Charles VII was a youth, northern France, including Paris, was taken from him and controlled by the English. From 1422 Charles was known mockingly as 'the little King of Bourges'. But in 1436 Paris was recaptured, although for some time Charles refused to go there and remained with his court in the Loire Valley. Alison's descriptions of preparations for a visit to Paris would seem not to refer to the King's initial entry to that city, but to a subsequent journey. The dates are clear from Alison's reference to the banishment of Louis, which took place in 1447. Alison says this is followed by a royal visit to Paris, on which Agnes is badly treated by the people of that city – and such an incident happened in 1448.

In the following section, Alison gets her dates right, reveals her own age, and her growing involvement with Jacques Coeur.

Bloxham: How old are you now?

Alison: About eighteen. (*Pause.*) If anything happened to my master, I wouldn't know what to do. He has looked after me so well, but he is frightened of this Louis – he is frightened of this Louis – frightened of what Louis will do now he has been banished from Court. He is frightened for the safety of the fair Agnes.

Bloxham: Now this is a little later. What is happening now?

Alison: We have had news. My master went to Paris and he came back and brought us news of Paris. When they rode in procession into Paris, the Queen rode with the King and then behind rode Agnes, and her two dogs were in

coats of white fur with jewelled collars. And the people
were spitting at her and saying that she is beautifully
dressed and even her pet dogs wear jewels and yet they
have no food.

And the Queen took her out on to the balcony, took Agnes
on to the balcony to show the people of Paris that she
loved Agnes and the people didn't shout at her any more.
No, the Queen is very cunning but she loves Agnes.

Bloxham: What else did your master tell you about Paris?

Alison: People are very poor and he said it was dirty. He is
very fussy, very clean.

Agnes Sorel certainly owned a pair of pampered pet dogs,
greyhounds 'Carpet' and 'Robin', who are lovingly referred to
in her letters. The Queen too was always friendly to Agnes in
public, although the King's love affair was an open secret.

Alison's version of the visit to Paris seems to be substantiated
by an account written at the time by the anonymous 'Citizen
of Paris'.

The last week in April, 1448, there came to Paris a damsel
who was said to be loved publicly by the King of France,
without faith and without law and without honour for the
good queen whom he had married, and it was apparent that
she maintained as great a state as a countess or duchess.

She went about generally with the good Queen of France
without regard for the scandal occasioned by her shame, on
account of which the Queen had much sorrow in her heart
but it was proper for her to bear it for the time being . . .
and she named herself and made others call her 'the beautiful Agnes' and because the people of Paris did not do her the
reverence demanded by her great pride she said, on depart-
ing, that they were just a rabble. . . .

Later Alison mentions that her master 'has gone to see
Agnes, she has had a child, a daughter. . . .' Altogether, in the
five years Agnes was the King's mistress she bore him four
daughters, three of whom survived.

But Agnes, the Maid of Fromenteau, was close to death when the fourth child was born in February 1449. This is how Alison describes those last days.

Alison: There is great anxiety – my master is very worried.

Bloxham: Is he?

Alison: Yes, very worried. The Maid of Fromenteau is dying. They don't know what is wrong with her. My master thinks she has been poisoned.

Bloxham: Oh!

Alison: My master thinks she has been poisoned.

Bloxham: Does he suspect anyone?

Alison: He suspects Louis, Louis de Valois. He suspects Louis, Louis is nowhere to be found.

Bloxham: Now this is a bit later. What is happening now?

Alison: The Maid of Fromenteau has died. (*Pause.*) The King is inconsolable, inconsolable. He is inconsolable. I am frightened for my master. I have heard the servants say that Louis is spreading the story that it was my master who killed Agnes. Louis hated Jacques Coeur. He hates Jacques Coeur and he's – I'm frightened they are going to harm my master. If they do what will happen to me? What will happen to me if they kill my master?

Bloxham: Your master hasn't had anything to do with it, has he?

Alison: Nothing at all. He loved Agnes. He was her true friend. He has had nothing to do with it at all, but they blame him.

Again Alison is correct. Today's historians debate whether Agnes Sorel was poisoned at all, some believe she died of an illness following the birth of her daughter. But fifteenth-century chroniclers shared Alison's suspicion that the King's mistress had been poisoned by the King's son, the Dauphin Louis. Jean du Clerq wrote:

She was hardly dead before they said she had been poisoned, and some also dared to assert that the dauphin had caused the death of the damsel named 'the Beautiful Agnes' who was entirely in the affections of his father the King.

Another chronicler, Monstrelet, wrote of 'the beautiful Agnes, against whom the dauphin had a great despite and, because of this hatred, he caused her death to be hastened.'

Alison's suspicions may have been shared by others in the fifteenth century, but her fears for Jacques Coeur's safety were well founded. The rumour that Coeur had poisoned Agnes was spread at court, false testimony about his involvement was given to the King, and in 1451 Coeur was imprisoned. This is Alison's version of Coeur's downfall and her own apparent death.

Bloxham : Well, this is later on. What is happening now ?
Alison : They are coming. The King has taken all wealth away from my master. What terrible gratitude, no gratitude. Taken his wealth – broken him and he supported the King in all that time. And he is saying that he believes Louis, that the master tried – well did poison the fair Agnes. (*Pause.*) But he didn't! He didn't! And the master is frightened that if the soldiers come here they might harm me, they might harm me. He wants me to go away. But I won't go. I won't go and leave him – I couldn't leave him. I'm staying here with him and when the soldiers come, soldiers come, I don't know what will happen. I don't want them to come. We've taken all we could possibly take before the King's men came and took our wealth – my master has given to a good friend to keep for him. He has broken us this King. What ingratitude! After all we did for him.
Bloxham : 'Put not your trust in princes.'
Alison : No, no, no. But my master was so good to the King, so good to the King.
Bloxham : I suppose he felt he couldn't repay him and so he stole the lot ?

Alison: No – I don't know. But it will be a sad day for France when Louis is on the throne. And it won't be long I think before Louis is on the throne.

Bloxham: Well, this is a bit later on. What is happening now?

Alison: It's black, black.

Bloxham: Did the soldiers come?

Alison: The soldiers came, the soldiers came.

Bloxham: And did they do anything to you?

Alison: No they didn't. My master gave me a draught and I went to sleep.

Bloxham: Did your master also take a draught?

Alison: No.

Bloxham: He didn't?

Alison: No.

Jacques Coeur did not 'take a draught'. He presented himself to the King in July 1451, at the castle of Taillebourg. He told the King he knew charges had been laid against him and that several of his 'subordinates had been forcibly laid hold of by royal command'. Coeur was thrown into a dungeon and his estates and possessions seized. He faced several charges including: poisoning Agnes, selling arms to the Arab infidels, exporting silver from France, conducting illegal dealings at the royal mint, and returning a Christian runaway slave to his Arab master. The trial began a year after his arrest and lasted ten months. The poisoning charge was dropped, but the others, almost equally unsubstantiated, went ahead.

The trial was a farce. The prosecutor was one of the judges and all three judges owed Coeur money they would never have to repay if he was found guilty. Coeur was not allowed to be represented nor to call witnesses. He was also 'put to the question' and tortured. Found guilty of five charges, he was forced to make the *amende honorable* – on his knees, bare headed, holding a lighted candle weighing ten pounds, he was made to confess his 'crimes' and beg for mercy. His life was spared, but he was banned from all public office, his wealth confiscated and he remained in prison.

But although Alison could know nothing of it, that was not quite the end of the Jacques Coeur story. Three years after his arrest, he managed to escape from prison and fled across France. On the border near the River Rhône, he was trapped by the King's men in a convent. They couldn't get at him and tried to poison him, but Coeur managed to send a message to some of his followers, including a few of his former sea captains. Eventually twenty armed men staged a midnight rescue and he escaped across the river.

Coeur went to Rome, where the Pope put him in charge of a fleet on a crusade against the Turks. On this expedition, off the coast of Asia Minor, Jacques Coeur, then aged sixty, died, possibly of wounds, in the year 1456.

To the many mysteries that surround the life of Coeur, we can now add another. Is it possible that this great French merchant prince was secretly in love with a young Arab girl he named Alison and who was kept quite apart from his wife and family? Alison's version of her own death seems to indicate a very special relationship with the man she served and was not prepared to leave or live without. Was she indeed Coeur's mistress, particularly in the year or so after the death of the King's mistress Agnes Sorel?

But if they were lovers, why should Coeur give Alison poison and not take it himself? Even this harsh act can have a reasonable explanation viewed against the times in which Coeur lived. Dislike of the infidel was so strong in Christian France that any Arab girl without the protection of the king's *argentier* would have faced a difficult future in the hands of the King's men. Her death might well have been an act of compassion.

Historically, of course, the main poisoning debate centres on whether Louis or Jacques Coeur might have poisoned the King's mistress Agnes Sorel. Alison suspected Louis, who had earlier been under suspicion of having poisoned his own wife, Margaret of Scotland. Was Louis a poisoner? History eventually added a grisly footnote to this debate, for in 1461 the ungrateful King Charles VII of France starved himself to death because he believed his son Louis was about to have him poisoned!

Chapter 8

SEARCH FOR A GOLDEN APPLE

A LISON'S story was, in some ways, the most impressive regression I had looked at. Her knowledge of fifteenth-century France existed on so many different levels.

As I moved around the castles and museums of the Loire Valley, talking to historians and curators who overwhelmed me with their offers of assistance, I began to realise just how very much Alison knew about medieval France. Apart from the historical outline of Jacques Coeur's life, which is what we have concentrated upon so far, Alison could talk copiously of the costume and dress of the period, she had a real knowledge of fifteenth-century painters, could describe Coeur's house at Bourges inside and out, and was familiar with objects he owned and collected.

All of this, for Bloxham's subject Jane Evans, is part of the story of Jacques Coeur, a long dead foreigner who lived in a place she has never visited. She says she had never heard his name before being regressed, and if her knowledge of him comes from a forgotten book, then it is an extremely scholarly work which I have so far been unable to trace.

I took with me to the Loire Valley the full Bloxham tape of Alison, including sections about Coeur's house and possessions we have not so far considered, and also a second tape. This was the sound track from the film of Jane Evans hypnotised and regressed as Alison.

This filmed experiment was not an unqualified success. The presence of a camera, lights and so many people in the room again created a tense atmosphere, and we seemed to run out of film at all the most critical moments.

The televised session was shorter than the original and,

although Alison's story was much as before, it was inevitably less detailed. Bloxham's subject assured me she had read nothing about Coeur since first being regressed five years earlier, but where Bloxham departed from his original line of questioning, sometimes at my prompting, we were given some extra information. A few of these snippets are worth mentioning.

After a first brief reference to the struggle between Charles VII, in the early years of his reign, and the Duke of Burgundy, Alison also gave some new background to a visit to Paris by the King.

> Alison: The King is having to be in Paris. (*Pause.*) He was not crowned in Paris – not Paris – someone else was crowned in Paris not Charles. (*Pause.*) The English, an English King, King of England and King of France.
> Bloxham: Which king is that?
> Alison: I think Henry – King of England, King of France. He was crowned in Paris.
> Bloxham: I see. You didn't see that did you?
> Alison: Oh no.

The King of England and France was Henry VI, who was crowned monarch of both countries in Paris in 1431. It took Charles years to win back Paris for the French throne. Consequently, as Alison said, Charles had been crowned 'not in Paris' but in Reims.

There is also new information about a successor to Agnes Sorel as the King's mistress.

> Bloxham: This is a little later. What is happening now?
> Alison: Agnes is dead. The King has another mistress.
> Bloxham: Oh, who is the King's new mistress?
> Alison: Her name is Antoinette. She is a cousin or half sister – she is related to Agnes – not as kind or good as Agnes. Bad effect on the King.

On the death of Agnes Sorel, King Charles took Antoinette de Maignelais for his mistress. She was said to be the niece of Agnes, but was never as popular a figure at the French court as her aunt.

Alison was next asked about painters. Her knowledge was impressive and there is no evidence of any equal familiarity with the arts in any of the other five regressions.

Alison: Artists have been here.
Bloxham: Who are the artists who come?
Alison: Painters.
Bloxham: Can you remember any of these?
Alison: I think – Fouquet. Yes, he is one who has been here.
Bloxham: Did he paint anything while he was here?
Alison: I can't remember.
Bloxham: Did he come to see your paintings?
Alison: No. He came to sell paintings to us. We bought paintings from him. He (Jacques Coeur?) collects fine paintings.
Bloxham: And what other painters have been here?
Alison: Van Eyck.
Bloxham: What did you think of Van Eyck?
Alison: I didn't see very much of him.
Bloxham: Didn't you?
Alison: He didn't come to see me.

'Fouquet' is unquestionably Jean Fouquet, born in 1420 and died in 1480. He was the court painter for Charles VII, and painted both the King and the royal mistress Agnes Sorel. He was also a personal acquaintance of Jacques Coeur, for receipts show that Fouquet, like so many others, borrowed money from Coeur.

Jan Van Eyck was also a contemporary. From 1425 until his death in 1441 Van Eyck was working in France as court painter to Philip the Good, Duke of Burgundy. Van Eyck travelled widely for the Duke and it is very possible he visited Bourges, particularly after 1435 when Philip and Charles VII patched up their quarrels and became allies.

But Alison talks about a specific painting of Agnes Sorel, with an infant as 'mother and child'.

Bloxham: Do you know which painter painted her?
Alison: Van Eyck.
Bloxham: You haven't got the painting of her have you, in the house?
Alison: No.
Bloxham: Who had the painting?
Alison: Réné. (Réné d'Anjou was the King's brother-in-law)

Van Eyck could have painted Agnes as a court beauty, she was nearly twenty when the Flemish master died. But more likely there is an interesting confusion in Alison's mind between Fouquet and Van Eyck, the two artists she says visited Coeur. A painting survives of Agnes with infant as 'Madonna and Child' by Jean Fouquet. It was painted shortly after the death of Agnes. The fact that she was dead, and Coeur's own close involvement with the King's mistress, might explain on sentimental grounds why Alison says her master was 'very anxious' to obtain this portrait.

Alison's knowledge of art is clear too in part of Bloxham's original tape.

Bloxham: Tell me more about your lovely house?
Alison: Many rooms, beautiful tapestries. And my master has one room that he takes me into occasionally where there is a long gallery with pictures. (*Pause*.) Pictures – beautiful pictures and he told me the names of some of the artists, beautiful pictures.
Bloxham: Can you remember the names of the artists?
Alison: Yes. John of Bruges, Van Eyck. I think (*pause*) Giotto.

It is already established that Coeur could have possessed a painting by Van Eyck, who was working for the nearby Duke of Burgundy. He could also have owned a work by the Italian master Giotto, who died a century before in 1337 – Coeur made a number of visits to Italy and was a wealthy and famous collector of art and objects of beauty.

It was the third name, 'John of Bruges', which had me baffled for a while. My reference books, of a non-specialist type, made no mention of such an artist. Eventually a librarian tracked him down from an entry in a book on art in German.

Little of his work survives, but he was a Flemish painter of miniatures who is known to have worked between the years 1368 and 1381. He was called alternatively 'John of Bruges' or John Bondolf.

And there is a credible link between this painter and Jacques Coeur. In the previous century, John of Bruges was a court painter in France to King Charles V. And this King was the grandfather of Charles VII, the 'King of Bourges' and patron of Jacques Coeur. It seems inevitable that some of this painter's work should have survived in Bourges.

Alison's ability to converse about art was not confined to painting. She tells Bloxham there were many statues in the house.

Bloxham: Which are the ones you remember most?
Alison: There are many. Animals and one of a dog, a hound.
Bloxham: Is it a special hound?
Alison: It's Agnes's hound.
Bloxham: Do you happen to know who carved it?
Alison: Someone from Italy – I don't know the name – the same man that did her tomb.
Bloxham: Oh, her tomb. What is her tomb like?
Alison: It is her.
Bloxham: Pardon?
Alison: It is her.
Bloxham: Oh, and where is the tomb?

Fig. 1. Clifford's Tower, York, where one hundred and fifty Jews were massacred in AD 1190. See Jane Evans' regression as Rebecca ('A Twelfth-century Jewess').

Fig. 2. Magnus Magnusson inside St Mary's Church, Castlegate, York, the possible scene of Rebecca's death. The problem was that no crypt was known to exist in the church when we visited it — six months later a workman discovered a crypt.

The leading figures of the Roman world in AD 286, who were all correctly named and described by Jane Evans as 'Livonia' (the Roman wife). Pictures by courtesy of the National Museum of Wales.

FATHER AND SON

Fig. 3. *Constantius.* According to Livonia, her husband Titus was tutor to Constantius's son at a villa in Eboracum (York) when Constantius was governor of Britain in the year 286. History does not record that Constantius was governor at this time, but there are remarkable gaps in history — there are missing years in the life of Constantius and no one knows who was governor of Britain at this time.

Fig. 4. *Constantine the Great* was the son of Constantius. Livonia says Constantine was her husband's pupil. Constantine's date of birth is unknown, but Livonia's version corresponds with the latest historical belief.

THE CONSPIRATORS

Fig. 5. *Carausius* — the Roman Admiral who plotted successfully to seize control of Britain but was murdered by his fellow conspirator — all accurately described by Livonia.

Fig. 6. *Allectus* — chancellor to Carausius and later his murderer, became ruler of Britain in his place. Livonia gives the historical facts and adds — 'I didn't like Allectus — he had cold eyes'.

Fig. 7. *Diocletian* became Emperor of Rome in 284 but decided to share his power. Livonia knew this and that Diocletian's daughter had married Galerius — part of a new plan to ensure the succession.

Fig. 8. *Maximianus* — invited to share power with Diocletian, persuaded Constantius to renounce his first wife Helena and marry Princess Theodora, daughter of the new joint emperor. Livonia describes the tragic consequences.

Fig. 9. An early Roman villa, possibly of the type referred to by Jane Evans in the Livonia regression.

Fig. 10, 11. Two views of Jacques Coeur's medieval home at Bourges, France, described by Jane Evans under hypnosis ('Search for a Golden Apple') — 'My master said that when he first had it built, it is a mixture of Byzantine — I think he said Byzantine — and Venetian architecture'

Fig. 12. Jacques Coeur, French merchant prince, described by Jane Evans ('A Servant in Medieval France') as 'medium height, thin, clever face, beautifully dressed'.

Fig. 13. The mystery woman of the Alison regression: Jacques Coeur's wife, Marée de Leodepard. Alison says she did not know Coeur was married.

Fig. 14. Charles VII, King of France, who accused Coeur of the murder of Agnes Sorel, the king's mistress. Alison says of the king that he had thin spindly legs 'with a long Valois nose'.

Fig. 15. Agnes Sorel died, believed poisoned, in 1449. Jacques Coeur was accused of her murder. Jane Evans as Alison reopens this historical mystery – 'He loved Agnes, he was her true friend. He has had nothing to do with it all, but they blame him.'

Fig. 16. Coeur after his trial was found not guilty of murder but forced to make the 'amende honorable': bareheaded, carrying a ten-pound lighted candle, confessing his sins.

Fig. 17. Louis of Valois, son of King Charles VII, was later King Louis XI. Alison says Louis was probably the real murderer of Agnes Sorel. She also suggests that Louis had earlier poisoned his own wife, Margaret of Scotland.

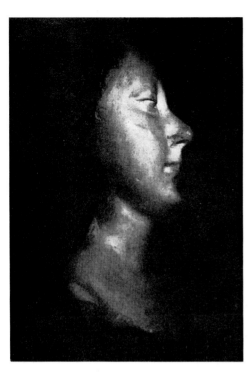

Fig. 18. The death mask of Agnes Sorel.

Fig. 19. The tomb of Agnes Sorel in the Château of Loches. When asked by the hypnotist to describe the tomb, Alison says 'It is her'.

Fig. 20. Catherine of Aragon, painted as a young girl before she left Spain to marry the English Prince Arthur. Under hypnosis, Jane Evans ('The Serving Girl and the Courtesan') says: 'We have to dress severely in the court— the Princess is very pious.'

Fig. 21. Arnall Bloxham with Graham Huxtable, who regressed as the gunner's mate in 'The Fight of HMS *Aggie*'. Huxtable's nautical beard has been grown since he was regressed as a sailor. Behind him is a Welsh bardic chair in carved oak which serves as Bloxham's hypnotist's couch.

Fig. 22. An eighteenth-century frigate of the probable period of Huxtable's regression.

Alison: In the church.

Bloxham: In the cathedral church you mean? (the cathedral church of Bourges)

Alison: No, not here – can't remember.

As Alison says, Agnes Sorel's tomb is 'her'. I visited the tomb in the castle of Loches. It has a reclining statue of Agnes with her hands together as if in prayer. The tomb has had a chequered history. It had been cast away by French revolutionaries and spent a hundred and sixty-five years, until its rediscovery in 1970, out of sight in a cellar. But in Alison's day the tomb, as she says, was in a church but not in Bourges – the church of St Ours at Loches. There it had remained until 1777, when it was started on its wanderings by priests who moved the tomb to a side aisle because it restricted their movements during services.

Today, nobody knows who sculpted the statue on the tomb. Alison's suggestion that it was by an Italian sculptor got some support from an historian in Bourges, M. Michel Bourgeois-Lechartier, who showed me a stone death mask of Agnes Sorel, known to have been made by an Italian artist. Might this Italian have been asked to sculpt the tomb? Could the death mask have been a preliminary for that major work?

As for a statue of 'Agnes's hound', most statues, paintings and fittings have long since vanished from Coeur's house. Many were smashed by French revolutionaries who saw them as symbols of aristocratic decadence. But Agnes had a known passion for her greyhounds 'Carpet' and 'Robin', and it is feasible one of her pets was carved in stone.

Enough evidence survives in *La Chaussée* to justify Alison's claim that Coeur had 'many statues' in his house. Towers and walls are inset with stone figures of men and animals, trees and ships, which survived presumably because they were out of easy reach of the revolutionaries.

Today, the house is labelled 'French gothic', a term unheard of in Coeur's day. The most obvious feature of the building is its two contrasting styles of architecture. From one side, it is

D

a castle, elegant with smooth tall towers and high windows. From the other, a masterpiece of ornamentation with arched doorways, decorated windows and walls and towers studded with statuary and intricate designs.

This clash between the fanciful and the functional seems to be appreciated by Alison, towards the end of her regression.

> Alison: This is said to be the only house in France with windows (glass windows were an innovation). It stands next door to the cathedral, near to the cathedral of Bourges. And my master said that, when he first had it built, it is a mixture of Byzantine – I think he said Byzantine – and Venetian architecture.
>
> Bloxham: That would look beautiful.
>
> Alison: Pointed doorways and sculptures over the doorways and big doors to come in, with big iron hooks hanging where we put the lanterns at night. And a courtyard – stone walls and tapestries – beautiful tapestries. And the floors are stone covered in carpets my master brought from the East and Persia.

The fittings may have gone, but there is still a large cobbled courtyard within the outer wall and the big gates. And the house itself is just a short walk away from the cathedral, if not exactly next door.

> Bloxham: Have you a lovely garden?
>
> Alison: Yes. Yes.
>
> Bloxham: Is there any water in the garden, a stream or anything like that?
>
> Alison: There is a fountain in the garden – a fountain.
>
> Bloxham: Do you like to spend time in the garden?
>
> Alison: No, I supervise the running of the house for my master, so that everything is left as he likes it.

Today there is no garden at *La Chaussée* but, as the guide books make clear, there was one in the fifteenth century, against the side of the house overlooking the countryside. Inside the house Alison accurately talks of high ceilings and large stone rooms and galleries; carvings, large furniture, ornate chairs and cushions after the Eastern fashion. She mentions a special room where Coeur kept his money and valuables. It was 'not in the house – hard to penetrate'.

At *La Chaussée*, this is an understatement. Jacques Coeur's 'treasure chamber' is near the top of a tall tower, up an interminable spiral staircase. The door is of solid iron and has seven locks and a peep-hole – definitely 'hard to penetrate'.

In the version of Alison's regression that we filmed there was another reference to the house. I prompted Bloxham to ask if Coeur had a coat of arms.

Alison: There is something about the fireplace. A shield, and I think animals and a shield by the fireplace. I can't see properly but there is a shield and animals on the shield.
Bloxham: Could you describe the animals on the shield?
Alison: No.
Bloxham: Is there a motto?
Alison: There's writing. Can't read. I can see it but I can't read it.

Jacques Coeur had his own coat of arms, but the device – hearts and scallop shells – did not include animals. However, in the main banqueting hall is a large fireplace about which are many carved stone animals. Alongside is the coat of arms of the King of France, which includes a shield and animals. On a side wall is Coeur's own motto, '*A vaillans coeurs rien impossible*' or 'to valiant hearts nothing is impossible'.

Much of Alison's detail fits *La Chaussée* very well, but the closest descriptions come later in the regression. The likelihood is that some of the earlier visits and events in Coeur's life, which Alison recalls, did not take place at *La Chaussée* but at another of the fine houses which Coeur owned in the same area. Not suspecting the existence of more than one house in

Bourges, Bloxham never asked questions which might have clarified the issue.

Coeur lived at Bourges for long periods throughout his life, but he did not begin to build his new house *La Chaussée* until 1443, and it was not ready even for part occupation for some years. The painter Van Eyck quite possibly visited Coeur in Bourges, but this could not have been at *La Chaussée*, since Van Eyck died in 1441, two years before the house was built!

That encounter must have taken place at one of Coeur's other houses. But the regression spans a total of almost ten years and before the end Alison seems clearly to be referring to Coeur's new mansion – she mentions the contrasting styles of architecture and is aware it is a newly built house – 'My master says that when he had it built....' But Coeur built other new houses in the Bourges district, so precisely where Alison claims she was living is uncertain. The answer would seem to be linked with her unawareness of Coeur's marriage. In the filmed version of the regression, Alison was again asked if Coeur had a family. Her reply was – 'No. Or if so I have not heard of them. He is on his own.'

And Coeur was a strangely secretive man. Historians have wondered if he was a poisoner. And what is the meaning of the 'joy' or 'love' referred to in inscriptions in Coeur's house, where everywhere carved and painted mottoes proclaim Coeur's golden rules of discretion, silence and never letting the right hand know what the left is up to.

Michelet wrote 'Coeur's house and life are full of mysteries'. And it would seem Alison's story is a mystery to add to the others. What is undeniable is that she knew some rare facts about the fifteenth-century Frenchman, as our search for 'a golden apple' demonstrated.

> Alison: And he has at the end of the passage with the portraits and pictures, he has a room where he keeps his porcelain and jade and he has a beautiful golden apple with jewels in it. He said it was given to him by the Sultan of Turkey.

Initially none of the historians and curators along the Loire Valley could identify this golden apple or anything like it. My colleague Magnus Magnusson produced an ingenious theory to show that a golden apple would have had a great appeal for Coeur, who delighted in puns and symbolic objects. Over Coeur's front door is a stone carving of an orange tree, a symbol of his trade with the Middle East, and the fifteenth-century French for an orange was *pomme d'or* or apple of gold.

This clever play on words seemed as close as we would get, until I arrived back at my hotel on the last night in Bourges. Waiting for me was a message from a historian, M. Pierre Bailly, – 'Monsieur, I think I have found your golden apple.'

In the archives, looking through what he termed 'an obscure list of items confiscated by the Treasury from Jacques Coeur', he came across an entry – a 'grenade' of gold. A grenade is a pomegranate, in shape and size so like an apple that the English term even contains the root word *pomme* or apple.

The object has probably long since been melted down – there was no reference to it having contained jewels when it was confiscated, for it was listed as 'salt cellar' – but the fact remains, Jacques Coeur had owned a golden apple!

Chapter 9

THE SEWING GIRL AND THE COURTESAN

THE final three regressions of Jane Evans show real changes of attitude and personality, but without the same marvellous wealth of historical detail as the 'lives' of Rebecca, Livonia and Alison.

The comparative lack of historical content was a mild disappointment, and yet it was a relief because, by the laws of averages, all six 'lives' of Jane Evans should not be centred around events from the pages of some obscure history book. Some of the lives, I felt, would surely be ordinary, not very dramatic, and so it was.

Two of the regressions are brief, and were recorded by Bloxham in the space of a single evening. A hypnotised Jane first became a strikingly diffident sewing girl in the London of Queen Anne. The girl had a personality distinct from that of any other regression. Bloxham managed to coax out only a handful of historical facts before the sewing girl found herself in an unpleasant room with fever victims. It was clear to Bloxham this very ordinary girl was not going to provide one of his 'interesting regressions' and so he woke her up.

Immediately afterwards, he rehypnotised Jane and regressed her back a further two hundred years to become a lady in waiting to the Infanta Catherina, preparing to set out from Spain to marry the English Prince Arthur in 1501. There is a good deal of verifiable historical fact in this regression, but it also ends suddenly when the girl became ill and apparently died.

Bloxham, anticipating a longer regression and trying to fit two 'lives' into the same evening, seemed to be pressed for time and did not question the girl as thoroughly as usual. Consequently in this regression Jane Evans is not as impressive historically as before, although the Spanish courtesan does show an interesting change of attitude towards sex, compared with Jane's other 'identities'.

Apart from Jane's final regression as the nun, the closest we come to the present day is in the 'life' of the sewing girl, around the year 1702.

This begins with the description of a dress, which Jane is sewing. But her name is Ann Tasker, she does not know her father, and lives with her mother in Paddington. With five other girls, Ann Tasker works for a seamstress in a large room in a London house.

This girl is young, possibly uneducated, works long hours and complains of being tired all the time. Her monosyllabic answers as Bloxham prises a few facts out of her contrast dramatically with the comparative fluency of the more mature characters of her earlier regressions. The change is worth studying – this really is a bored teenager!

Bloxham: Do you know if there is a king or a queen?
Ann: A queen.
Bloxham: Which queen is this?
Ann: Queen Anne.
Bloxham: Yes, I see.
Ann (*flatly*): Fat lady.
Bloxham: Have you seen Queen Anne?
Ann: No.
Bloxham: Are you married?
Ann: No.
Bloxham: Have you a friend or lover?
Ann: No.
Bloxham: How old are you?
Ann: I think about seventeen.
Bloxham: Have you brothers or sisters?
Ann: Yes.
Bloxham: How many?
Ann: Two.

Bloxham: Are they older or younger?

Ann: Older.

Bloxham: What do they do?

Ann: They're in the army.

Bloxham: They're not fighting though, are they?

Ann: They're away.

Bloxham: Are they fighting against any country?

Ann: I think they're in France.

Bloxham: In France? Are they fighting?

Ann: Yes.

Bloxham: Who are they fighting?

Ann: They're in France – they're with Marlborough.

Bloxham: With Marlborough?

Ann: Yes. They call him Marlborough.

Bloxham: I see. Did you see your brothers in their uniform?

Ann: No.

Bloxham: Have you seen any very special people or made clothes for them?

Ann: No.

Bloxham: You haven't? What special events have taken place.

Ann: They had a parade for the Duke of Gloucester.

Bloxham: For the Duke of Gloucester?

Ann: The Duke of Gloucester has died – he was the only child of Queen Anne and they had a special funeral for him.

Bloxham: They had a special funeral?

Ann: Yes.

Bloxham: Did you see this funeral?

Ann: No. I couldn't get near.

Bloxham: You couldn't get near. Didn't you see any of the parade?

Ann: Not much.

Bloxham: Where did you go to see it?

Ann: I went to town.

Bloxham: Do you know which street you were in?

Ann: No.

Bloxham: You don't?
Ann: A lot of us went.
Bloxham: Were you very sad?
Ann: No. (*Pause.*) I didn't know him.

This girl's manner and attitude towards Bloxham are quite unlike any of the other regressions, and her personality is not recognisably that of Jane Evans. Anyone who has ever tried to question an unresponsive teenager will appreciate the difficulty Bloxham has in getting information from this girl. She knows certain facts but they have to be dragged out of her by a series of direct questions.

Historically what she says is accurate. Queen Anne was crowned on 8 March 1702, and in May of that year the war of the Spanish Succession began and the British Army was soon in Europe to fight the French. British soldiers were there for years, and, as the girl says, the Duke of Marlborough was the Captain General of British troops at home and abroad, and was soon to lead the Anglo-Dutch army to notable victories against the French.

Eighteen months before the outbreak of this war, London had seen the state funeral of the Duke of Gloucester, who died aged eleven years. As the sewing girl said, this prince had been the only child of Queen Anne.

Bloxham's subject then introduced the only other personality named in this regression. A rich lady had called at the workroom for a dress.

Bloxham: What was the name of the lady who came today?
Ann: I don't know – I think it was something like Villiers.
Bloxham: Villiers? Lady Villiers?
Ann: I think so – yes, Villiers – the lady with red hair and funny eyes.
Bloxham: They were funny eyes were they?
Ann: Yes. She had a squint.
Bloxham: Oh really?
Ann: Yes – I'm sure her name was Villiers.

Bloxham: What else did Lady Villiers say?

Ann: Nothing to me – I'm just somebody who sews on the beads.

Bloxham: You sew on the beads? Do you like that?

Ann: It's tiring – my eyes ache.

Bloxham: What colour beads do you sew on?

Ann: Pearl – I'm not allowed to sew on real pearls – only Margaret sews on real pearls.

Historically, the lady with the red hair could have been either Barbara Villiers, Duchess of Cleveland, or a relative. Barbara Villiers, who lived from 1641 until 1709, was a former mistress of King Charles II – a celebrated lady, she once had an affair with the Duke of Marlborough, in his earlier days as John Churchill.

The regression of the sewing girl is almost finished. Bloxham, perhaps exasperated by Ann Tasker's offhand manner, moves his subject forward in time.

Bloxham: Now this is a bit later. What are you doing now?

Ann: I'm in a dirty, filthy room – people are sick.

Bloxham: Are they? Oh dear, is it a tavern?

Ann: No – terrible smell, filthy room, people are sick, rolling, sick.

Bloxham: Have they been drinking?

Ann: No. Sick.

Bloxham: They're just ill? Oh dear, is it some sort of plague or something?

Ann: There's always a plague where I live – the filth and the smell and the stench, it's awful – people don't wash.

Bloxham: Are they really ill these people?

Ann: It's fever – hot – smell – stench, foul mess. . . .

Bloxham: I am going to wake you up. . . .

Jane Evans woke up saying: 'I'm tingling, there's a terrible smell.' Bloxham explained: 'This one isn't a very nice one so I woke you up. Anyhow, I'll do another one of you if you like.'

And so she was hypnotised again and described a scene in a courtyard where men and horses are preparing for a journey. The men are dressed in 'slashed hose and doublets with puffed sleeves'. The date would seem to be May 1501, and the Spanish Infanta Catherine is about to leave to marry Prince Arthur of England. Jane Evans is a lady in waiting named Anna.

> Bloxham: Will you tell me what the Infanta looks like?
> Anna: Plump, plain but very nice.
> Bloxham: What does she call you?
> Anna: Anna.
> Bloxham: Are you dark or fair?
> Anna: The same as the Infanta Catherina – in between dark and fair – no definite colour.

The descriptions of Catherine, who had brown hair, fit the facts. Anna said 'plump and plain', later in England she would be called: 'Rather ugly than otherwise; of low stature and rather stout; and very religious.' The anglicised form of the Infanta's name is Catherine, but 'Catherina' is closer to the original Spanish, especially since Anna pronounces it 'Katarina'.

Anna says correctly that the Infanta's parents are King Ferdinand and Queen Isabella. Her own parents are from Madrid and Anna says her last name is 'of Castile'. This has a logical sound, since Queen Isabella was ruler of Castile in her own right and might well have chosen, as a companion for the Infanta, some relative from her own royal house. Madrid, not yet the capital of Spain, was an important town in Castile, and the court would certainly live there from time to time.

> Bloxham: Is anything very special going on at the present time?
> Anna: The marriage of the Infanta Catherina – she's going to England.
> Bloxham: Who is she going to marry?
> Anna: Prince Arthur.

Bloxham: Will you go with her?

Anna: Yes.

Bloxham: And what are the horsemen doing in the courtyard?

Anna: They are waiting to take us.

Bloxham: So you are very excited I expect?

Anna: No. The Infanta is crying – she doesn't want to leave
the queen – oh no she doesn't want to go to England.

Bloxham: And what does the queen think about it?

Anna: Very sad – all the children have married.

Bloxham: How old is the Infanta?

Anna: Seventeen or eighteen.

Bloxham: How old are you?

Anna: The same age.

Bloxham: It must be nice for you living at court?

Anna: It was a happy place but not any more. The queen
is sad – all the children are married except the Infanta –
and now she must go to that cold, wet England – she
doesn't want to go.

Bloxham: Who arranged the marriage?

Anna: King Ferdinand – with the King of England.

Bloxham: Who is the King of England?

Anna: I think it is Henry – yes, Henry – we have heard that
Arthur is weak – Prince Arthur is weak.

Except that the Infanta is almost sixteen years old and not
seventeen, Anna has got the facts right. King Ferdinand of
Aragon and King Henry VII of England had arranged the
marriage – the young couple were pledged to each other when
Catherine was three years old and Prince Arthur was two!

The Infanta, as Anna said, was the youngest of the five
children of Ferdinand and Isabella and she was the only one
left at court. Her three sisters had married and her brother
Juan had died. The reluctance of Queen Isabella to part with
her youngest daughter was also very real, and she delayed
sending Catherine to England as long as possible.

In 1501 the Spanish court was a gloomy place. Since the

death of the Spanish heir Prince Juan, the queen had turned increasingly towards her religion. Isabella had always been a fanatical Catholic. She had ridden in armour with her knights on Crusades as a younger woman, and now she dressed only in black and underneath wore the habit of a nun. Catherine, educated by her mother, shared her faith and attitudes.

By comparison Anna was a giddy, promiscuous teenager. For the first time in the regressions, Jane Evans is a woman with 'many lovers', who complains that the *duennas*, or older women who act as chaperones and governesses, keep too close a watch on her!

Bloxham: How do you usually dress?

Anna: We have to dress severely in the court – dark colours.

Bloxham: Otherwise you would look prettier than the princess?

Anna: The princess too – we are all severe. We had somebody here from France and somebody from Portugal at the other weddings and their fashions were different to ours – far prettier.

Bloxham: Do you wear jewellery?

Anna: No.

Bloxham: Aren't you allowed to?

Anna: The Infanta is very pious.

Bloxham: Are you very pious?

Anna: When I have to be.

Bloxham: Do you have to go to confession?

Anna: Yes – when the Infanta goes, we have to go.

Bloxham: What have you done that you didn't tell the priest?

Anna: We are not supposed to have men, but we do.

Bloxham: Do you think the Infanta knows?

Anna: Oh no – she would be very shocked.

The regression moves to the point of departure. It is recorded that Queen Isabella did not accompany her daughter on the three months long journey through Spain to the coast, because she was too busy supressing a revolt by the Moors in Granada.

Anna, asked by Bloxham if the queen is to go with them to the sea, says: 'No. Only part of the way on the journey.'

For her journey to England, the Infanta's retinue included an archbishop, a personal priest, a chamberlain, a marshal, a butler, maids of honour, page boys, hairdressers and cooks – sixty persons in all.

The land journey and the sea crossing are described only briefly in the regression, partly because Anna complained of feeling so unwell aboard ship that Bloxham felt obliged to move the regression forward.

> Anna: – terrible storms – the Infanta is crying.
> Bloxham: Are you giving her comfort?
> Anna: I am sick and crying too – rolling – rolling – rolling.
> Bloxham: Are all the court ill too?
> Anna: Oh yes.
> Bloxham: Now this is later on – where are you now?
> Anna: Going along the road. . . .

The crossing from Spain to England had been very stormy. Six weeks after setting sail, and at the second attempt, the Spanish fleet finally landed at Plymouth Hoe on 2 October 1501.

Anna, asked by Bloxham if Dover was the port they sailed into, replied – 'Dover, Dover, I heard Dover but I don't think it was Dover. It's a funny named place – I can't remember.'

When the overdue Spaniards finally struggled into Plymouth, no royal messenger was there to meet them. The first delegation from the English court called on the Infanta in Exeter two weeks after their arrival. In the meantime, they had been made warmly welcome by the people of the West Country.

> Bloxham: What did you do when you landed?
> Anna: It was raining – terrible – raining – damp. There were
>   people to meet us, but we were told the king was coming

to meet the Infanta – but he wasn't there. He's supposed
to meet us on the way to London, with the Prince Arthur.

Bloxham: I expect you look very decorative don't you?

Anna: No – we're plainly dressed. The other women that
came with the people to meet us are very fancy, but we
are plain – dark – very plain clothes compared with the
clothes they have got. The Infanta is rather shocked.

Bloxham: She thinks you ought to have more gay clothes?

Anna: She thinks that their clothing should be more modest!

History records that the king finally met his Spanish guests
at the Bishop of Bath's Palace at Dogmersfield, 'fifteen leagues
from London'. Prince Arthur was there too, aged fifteen, 'half
a head shorter than the princess, slim, fair skin, pale as snow'.

Prince Henry was then ten years old and already bigger than
his brother Arthur. Eight years later and he was to marry the
Infanta himself and to become Henry VIII. Anna seems to
know something of this early meeting.

Bloxham: How long did you stay at the English court?

Anna: We are not in the English court – we stayed in a
house, a big house, outside London.

Bloxham: And what is happening there?

Anna: They are going to send me back – a lot of us are
going back to Spain.

Bloxham: Did you meet the king?

Anna: We saw him and we saw Prince Arthur – very pale
– his brother Henry was handsome, very curly hair –
curly haired Henry with red hair. But Arthur looked weak
and pale – the Infanta is so youthful and well – he looks
pale and small beside her.

A month later, in December 1501, Catherine of Aragon and
Prince Arthur were married. She was aged sixteen and he was
fifteen. Arthur was Prince of Wales and that winter the very
young couple moved to the principality. By April Arthur was
dead, it is presumed either of the plague or of consumption.

Anna, it would seem, was one of those intended to return to Spain along with the Archbishop of Santiago, who set out soon after the wedding.

Bloxham: Now you are back on the coast – did you have to stay in any house before boarding your ship?

Anna: We stayed at inns.

Bloxham: Do you know what inns you stayed at?

Anna: No. It was dark when we arrived and it was raining, as it is always raining.

Bloxham: Can you tell me the name of your ship?

Anna: No.

Bloxham: Weren't you very interested?

Anna: I was too ill – sick.

Bloxham: But you'll probably not be sick upon this return?

Anna: No – I feel ill – hot – my head's aching – hot.

Bloxham: After the journey?

Anna: Yes, but hot and head is aching – sick.

Bloxham: Who is looking after you?

Anna: They've sent for a doctor – putting things on my head – to stop the fever – I'm still hot – I'm hot, it's so hot.

Bloxham: This is a bit later – are you feeling better?

Anna: Still hot, dark.

At this point in the regression, Bloxham woke Jane Evans. We shall never know if Anna saw her parents or Spain again.

Chapter 10

THE AMERICAN NUN

THE sixth and final regression of Jane Evans is very different from any of the others. She lives in modern times, is possibly alive until as late as 1920, and is a nun in America.

This was by far the most recent of the 'previous lives' and, on the face of it, should have been the easiest to corroborate. It didn't turn out like that, because Sister Grace, vague and other-worldly, spends her entire adult life within the confines of a convent. This American nun, all too human and rather sad, a misfit in religious life, is poor material for researchers and historians. In stark contrast to most of her other regressions, Jane Evans as the nun is almost totally unaware of ordinary events in the outside world.

But there are points of real interest. For a start, Jane Evans had never been to America when she recorded this regression. She was also brought up a Nonconformist, attended a Presbyterian Sunday School and says she knows nothing about Roman Catholicism or nuns.

In the regression, Sister Grace says her childhood was spent in Des Moines, which is a city in the State of Iowa. She mentions a street, a 'Route Two', which actually seemed to exist there last century. She gives her surname as 'Ellis', which is not the most common of names – but seems to be strongly represented in Des Moines both in the last century and today. There are a few dozen Ellises in the latest telephone directory and, more important, in the middle of last century, when Des Moines was not much more than a fast-growing village of a few hundred families, we have so far traced a dozen people named Ellis. The Ellis clan seemed to have settled in Des

Moines in some force, although the nun's actual family has not been positively identified.

One problem is that 'Grace' is almost certainly not the name by which Miss Ellis would have been known in Des Moines last century. Grace would be the name given to her on entering the convent, to symbolise her new 'spiritual identity'.

Additionally, it is never clear in the regression how many years of her childhood were spent in Des Moines or whether her mother lived on in that town after her daughter left for the convent. Checking birth certificates would be of little use, since registration of births in Iowa did not become compulsory until the 1920s. There were a number of censuses taken towards the end of the last century, although the lady in the census bureau told me that 'these censuses are not a hundred percent; people appear in one, they're off the next, but they were still living round here.'

From the censuses, numerous families of Ellis and one of 'Ellice' have been uncovered. Apart from ordinary gaps in the record, there's one rather more spectacular: the federal or national census for the year 1890 in Iowa was ordered to be destroyed by the government in Washington because it had been partly damaged by a fire. The Federal Census was taken every ten years from 1860 and there is a twenty-year gap from 1880 to 1900.

Tracing the elusive Sister Grace through the records of American religion is another daunting task. There are numerous religious orders and many thousands of nuns in America. The verifiable information that Sister Grace gives about her order is scant, but she could belong to the Sisters of Mercy, which she seems to name. There are more than ten thousand Sisters of Mercy spread across America, and last century they existed in scores of scattered and independent convents.

At the mother house in Maryland, Sister Mary Felicitas has spent hours searching through some of the archives. To cheer me up, she told me on the telephone – 'Don't worry, I never give up on a problem. Only last week I found an answer I'd been seeking for twenty-eight years!'

Sister Grace's lack of factual awareness in the regression, irritating to the researcher, made an interesting contrast with Jane Evans herself. The nun, struggling to think of anything she knew about the First World War, did not seem able to call upon the historical facts Jane Evans had learned at school or been told by her father, who was a soldier. The nun's awareness and Jane Evans's memory did not seem to be closely linked.

Taken at face value, Sister Grace's story makes gentle reading. A young woman, full of doubts and imagined sins, rebels mildly against convent life – she eats too much, sings tunelessly, and runs and laughs. Only in old age, crippled by arthritis, does she attain a sort of tranquillity – 'they like me and that's all I care.'

There is a clear maturing of personality from the uncertainty of the young woman to the longer speeches and more firmly held heresies of the older nun. The script reads like pages from a rather sad diary, and at least one of my colleagues says it's her favourite of the Jane Evans regressions. But until I can positively identify Sister Grace, it won't be mine.

Interestingly, Jane Evans, in earlier life, also suffered from arthritis, although nothing like as severely as Sister Grace.

The regression begins with Jane Evans whispering that she can see 'pillars – a lot of pillars with arches – it's dark in there.'

Bloxham: Are they very high pillars?

Grace: No. It's (*Pause.*) it's a walk.

Bloxham: It's a walk – oh yes.

Grace (*voice full of suprise*): It's – it's a long walk. It's – there are people going – there are people – a lot of people now – in procession.

Bloxham: In procession?

Grace: In procession, two at a time.

Bloxham: How are they dressed?

Grace: They are nuns (*Pause.*) and I can hear a bell.

Bloxham: Is it tolling?

Grace: Yes. Yes. And I can see the ambulatory.

An ambulatory was a cloister, an arched area for walking, usually found in monasteries and convents.

Bloxham: What is this occasion?
Grace: It's prayers. (*Pause.*) And they are hurrying.
Bloxham: Are you in this procession?
Grace: Yes.
Bloxham: What is your name? What do they call you?
Grace: Grace.
Bloxham: How old are you?
Grace: Young.
Bloxham: Are you a novice?
Grace: No.
Bloxham: Are you in black too?
Grace: Yes – no. No. It's not black – it's – it's grey. (*Pause.*) I've got a ring on my hand – a ring, a ring on my hand.
Bloxham: Which hand?
Grace: My left hand.

The ring on the left hand symbolised a nun's spiritual marriage. The reference to Sister Grace's habit being 'grey' – which she said in a rather startled way as if she had just looked down – I took at first to mean automatically that she belonged to an order of nuns who wore that colour. There are several of these, including the Sisters of the Sacred Heart.

But later Grace makes it clear she works in the kitchens, and in most orders, including the Sisters of Mercy, nuns who worked in the kitchens, the bakeries or perhaps the hospital, wore white – a colour which perhaps can sometimes be mistaken for grey.

In the last century, the Sisters of Mercy normally wore black. At no stage in the regression does Grace tell us the colour of the habits of the other nuns.

Bloxham: Have you a cross?
Grace: Oh yes. We all have crosses.

Bloxham: What is your cross made of?

Grace: I think it's ivory.

Bloxham: Are you happy as a nun?

Grace: Oh yes.

Bloxham: What do you do particularly as a nun?

Grace: I'm in the kitchen. I've got a box – a box with herbs – I grow herbs.

Bloxham: What sort of food do you cook in the kitchen?

Grace: All sorts of food – not just plain food – not plain food – we like food with herbs and I grow herbs.

Bloxham: Do you make bread?

Grace: Not me. Not me. One of the other nuns makes bread.

Bloxham: How long have you been a nun?

Grace: A long time – no, not so long really. It seems a long time.

Bloxham: What is the name of the Mother Superior?

Grace: I know her as Mother Superior. I don't know her name – she is just 'Mother Superior'.

Bloxham: What is she like?

Grace: Ageless. Ageless.

Bloxham: Are they very strict?

Grace: Yes. Yes. We all have penances. We all have penances.

Bloxham: Do you mind having penances?

Grace: Not if I've done wrong and I have to have a penance. But they give penances for things that before weren't wrong.

Bloxham: What do they give a penance for?

Grace: Well, we have to tell them if we think we have sinned, whereas before – before being a nun – it wouldn't be a sin. But when you are a nun it's a sin. It doesn't seem right somehow.

Bloxham: Do any Fathers come to visit you?

Grace: Priests come – priests come – yes.

Bloxham: Did you have to confess anything?

Grace: No – except I eat more than I should eat – but is that a confession?

Bloxham: You have to confess that, do you?

Grace: Well, I suppose it's an 'indulgence of the body'.

Bloxham: What did your father do?

Grace: My father was – I don't know – I can't remember my father. I can't remember my father.

Bloxham: Did he die when you were young?

Grace: Yes – my mother brought us up.

Bloxham: Had you brothers or sisters.

Grace: No. I had a small brother who died. Then just my mother and I.

Bloxham: What was the name of the place where you lived?

Grace: Maryland – no – Maryland, Maryland is in my mind. It wasn't Maryland – wasn't Maryland.

Bloxham: What was your father's name?

Grace: Ellis.

Bloxham: Do you know where your family came from?

Grace: My mother said they came from England.

Bloxham: Who was the king of England when you were outside in the world?

Grace: It wasn't a king – it was a queen – Victoria.

Bloxham: And who was the President of America?

Grace (*pause*): I can't remember.

This inability to recall who was President, whilst remembering the name of the Queen of England, is perhaps forgivable because Victoria reigned for sixty-four years, from 1837 until 1901, during which time a dozen Presidents came and went.

Bloxham: Why did you decide to become a nun?

Grace: My mother wanted it – my family were strong Catholics – Catholics.

Bloxham: Wouldn't you have liked to marry?

Grace: I was never given an opportunity – I was always – my mother always wanted me to be a nun – and I was young.

Bloxham: Are you a pretty woman?

Grace: I don't know – it's a sin.

Bloxham: What events have taken place lately?

Grace: We had somebody here – a lady here – who came into retreat. That was interesting – although we are not supposed to look at them or talk to them – but that was interesting – she was very lovely.

Bloxham: Are there any jealousies among the nuns?

Grace: Oh yes. There are jealousies amongst women – always amongst women – petty things, petty things.

Bloxham: Have you got a friend?

Grace: Marguerite, Marguerite – she is a cook.

Bloxham: Is she?

Grace: Very fat – very fat! (*Pause.*) We make our interests. We garden – we have beautiful gardens – we grow our vegetables and I have my herbs.

Bloxham: Which are you specially fond of?

Grace: I like basil – and thyme – all of them. I put them in food but their smell alone is beautiful – it makes a change from the smell of old fusty cloth and damp places.

Bloxham: Is your nunnery damp?

Grace: Quite damp – in the chapels – yes.

Bloxham: Where is your convent situated?

Grace: Well, Maryland is in my mind but I don't think it's Maryland. I don't think it's Maryland.

Bloxham: Can you tell me where you used to live?

Grace: Des Moines.

Bloxham: Can you remember the name of the street?

Grace: Not a street – not a street – it was outside – we had – it was a route – Route Two, Des Moines.

Bloxham (*misunderstanding*): Route to Des Moines.

Grace: No – Route Two, Des Moines.

Bloxham: What was your father's Christian name?

Grace: Clarence.

Bloxham: And your mother's Christian name?

Grace: Irma.

Last century, Des Moines was a fast growing town on the

junction of the Raccoon and Des Moines rivers. In 1851 it had just five hundred inhabitants – six years later it had grown to become the state capital, replacing Iowa City.

There was a large influx of population and, from the census returns for 1860 and 1870, a fair proportion of them were named Ellis: for instance, 'Severs Ellis' is listed in 1860 as having a daughter, S. H. Ellis, aged one year. But none of the entries refer to a street or road, they simply mention the parish in which the person lives, in this case 'Cedar township', a part of Des Moines; and sometimes only a person's initials, instead of Christian names, are given.

Earlier in the regression, the nun makes it clear she was brought up by her mother alone – so Clarence Ellis is not in the picture.

It is interesting too that Des Moines in the nineteenth century was a town where Mother M. Francis Xavier established one of thirty-nine convents for the Sisters of Mercy in America.

If the nun's story is true, what could be more natural than for her mother to place her with a religious order which already had a convent in the town, and where perhaps she might have sought advice about her daughter's future?

Bloxham: Have you seen your mother since you became a nun?

Grace: She came once when I was ill – my joints – my joints – they called it rheumatism – my joints in my arms and my legs. My mother came – I was swollen – my hands are bent a little.

Bloxham: How old are you now?

Grace: Thirty – thirty-five – time passes in time – you don't realise – I don't realise the time passes.

Bloxham: Do you have news of the outside world?

Grace: Yes – the sisters go out – some sisters go out – I have been, but not lately. I want to go but they won't send me – I think – ah – I think they fear for my spiritual welfare.

Bloxham: Do they?

Grace (*laughs gently*): People – I'm interested in people.

Sometimes I feel I want to run up to the gates and I want to bang the doors and I want to go out because I want to see people – I want to see people.

Bloxham: And to talk?

Grace: To talk to people – yes – talk to children – people – anything. They fear for my spiritual welfare.

Bloxham: They think you wouldn't come back?

Grace: Oh, I'd come back – but they fear for me sometimes I think. Yes, I have thoughts sometimes – I have thoughts of people – I love people – people who can talk – people who can talk to me – discuss, debate, argue – not just pray and wander round – and pray and wander round.

Bloxham: It's a bit aimless isn't it?

Grace (*vehemently*): Yes, but it's sinful to think otherwise – it's sinful of me – I shouldn't think like this – I shouldn't think – Mother Superior knows I think like this.

Bloxham: Has she told you about it?

Grace: Yes. Yes. She's asked me – she has asked me – I haven't seen her much but she did ask me how I felt.

Bloxham: Is the Mother Superior Irish perhaps?

Grace: No. No. She's American.

Bloxham: Have you any coloured nuns there?

Grace: No. No. Ordinary girls – ordinary girls – I sometimes think – although it's not right to think – that they're here because there's nothing much for them to do anywhere else. Some of them – some of them can hardly read and write – some of them are bad – some of them I can't understand – have no vocation. (*Pause.*) I have no – I don't think I have a vocation – I don't think I have a vocation.

Bloxham: Are there any very saintly nuns here?

Grace: Yes – 'when the golden bowl shall shatter and the silver cord shall break' – yes.

Grace is quoting here from the passage in Ecclesiastes (Chapter 12 verse 6) in the Bible, which ends with the words, 'Vanity, vanity, saith the preacher, all is vanity.' But she seems also to have in mind the belief expressed in some religious writings that an angel's halo was held by a silver cord.

Bloxham: What does that mean?

Grace: I was thinking of saintly nuns – saintly nuns – yes – and their haloes.

Bloxham: Have you ever had a very spiritual experience?

Grace: I don't know – I was once in the chapel on my own and it went terribly cold – terrible cold and I felt as if there was somebody there – but that's all – and there was nobody there. But I felt something and I feel this all around here and sometimes I get frightened because I feel things. I sense – I can look at some of the other nuns and I can sense things. I can sometimes know what they are thinking.

Bloxham: It must be very embarrassing for them.

Grace: Well some of them are too saintly to live – yes – they have a horror of me I think. I'm a little different, a little different – in fact a great deal different to most of them.

Bloxham: Because you are still interested in the outside world?

Grace: Yes. Yes.

Bloxham: Have you heard any news from the outside world that made you feel you would like to go out into the world?

Grace: No. No. There have been – there was a war – there was a war – I heard there was a war but we don't hear much. It was in – I think – I think it was something about a desert – war in a desert – war in a desert I think – yes.

Bloxham: Who was fighting?

Grace: I don't know. I don't know.

This reference could be to any of several wars last century. Interestingly, the present-day Jane Evans could talk more convincingly about most of these than when regressed as Sister Grace. In America, the Apache wars in Arizona were fought 'in a desert' and ended in 1886 with the surrender of Geronimo. That other American conflict, the brief war with Spain in 1898, lasting only 114 days with land fighting confined to Cuba and the Philippines, could hardly be described as a 'desert' war. But another possibility is the British struggle with the Dervishes in the Sudan in the 1880s, which included the much publicised fall of Khartoum and death of General Gordon in 1885. Later in the century, the British were involved in a three-years war with the Boers in South Africa from 1899. But the most likely locations for this 'war in a desert' would seem to be Arizona or the Sudan.

Bloxham: I expect you would have liked to have heard more about it?

Grace: Yes. Yes. I'd like to have newspapers – newspapers and books. We have books here, but only the convent books – only the ecclesiastical books.

Bloxham: Have you any beautifully illuminated books?

Grace: Yes. Yes. We have a little novice who dusts and cleans them – dusts and cleans them – there's one big book with a lock – a lock and gold figure work on the front – and beautiful filigree work on the front – a big leather book – with beautiful gold on it – beautiful things.

Bloxham: Do you know who did this book?

Grace: No. No. I don't see much of the books because I'm only in the kitchens, but I would like to see the books – I'd like to see the books. I have to – I have been sinful in these things – wanting books, newspapers – I will have to confess – I think sometimes I must shock the priest and Mother Superior – they must think – no wonder they worry about my spiritual welfare – I shock them occasionally – I run and I laugh.

Bloxham: Do you like shocking them?

Grace: Yes. Yes. (*Pause.*) I run, and I laugh when I shouldn't laugh, and I sing tunelessly – I sing.

Bloxham: What do you like to sing?

Grace: Well, I just hum things I make up – I'm not really
supposed to – only when we're chanting – we don't do
much. But I like to sing – I like to hum old things that I
knew at home.

Bloxham: What songs did you know at home?

Grace: Oh, old negro spirituals that we all knew – spirituals
– 'Oh golden slippers' I remember. . . . (*Grace sings
quietly*.) 'Oh dem golden slippers – Oh dem golden slippers'. Yes, we used – my mother used to sing it to me –
yes.

'Oh dem golden slippers' is the first line of a quite well
known traditional negro spiritual.

Bloxham: You have a nice voice?

Grace: Oh they don't think so – no, they think I sing out
of tune. To me I sound beautiful – to me my voice is
beautiful, but to them – it's tuneless they say. Yes, they
laugh at me, but if I can make somebody laugh that's
something.

Bloxham: Who is the priest who comes to see you here,
to hear confession?

Grace: Ignatius – Father Ignatius. He's tall – a tall, pale,
ascetic type of man – pale.

Bloxham: Do you think he's Italian or Spanish?

Grace: I don't know – he just speaks the same as everybody
else – he sounds the same as everybody else.

Bloxham: Is he attractive?

Grace: I don't find him so.

Bloxham: Do the other nuns?

Grace: I've never heard them say – but then it's a sin to
find men attractive – even Father Ignatius.

Bloxham: When you confess things to Father Ignatius,
what does he say?

Grace: I haven't had anything much – serious – to confess
really. Except I overeat – a lot of us overeat – we feed
very well. But I don't – except perhaps I've been late –

I've been late for prayers – but he's always very kind.

Bloxham: Have any of the nuns been very ill lately?

Grace: Only me. I didn't know what it was – I was swollen – terribly swollen – my legs and arms. But I seemed to get better – they all prayed for me and that was supposed to have done it – I hadn't been feeling well for a long time and then suddenly I was swollen and in pain – terrible pain – oh for a long time I couldn't move or hardly move. But it was so lonely because they all had their duties to do – I was all on my own. And anyway I'm better so I must thank God. I'm better and I'm able to do things now – but my hand, my one hand, my left hand, my finger with my ring is big, swollen – my both hands are bad, not as bad – thank God – as they were.

Bloxham: Now this is later on – have you heard any news lately from the outside world?

Grace: Yes. There's a war – we're not in it – we're not in it – Germany and Britain at war – they're at war we've heard – we heard they're at war.

Bloxham: Do you know what year this is?

Grace: It must be – it must be 1914–15 – I think it must be. I remember that one of the sisters said it was something 1914–15 – I'm crippled now.

Britain and Germany began the war in 1914 and America did not enter until 1916.

Bloxham: You're crippled?

Grace: Yes I'm crippled – my hands and my legs are crippled – terrible pain – dreadful pain – people are kind – very kind – but I'm crippled.

Bloxham: Do you know at what place this convent is?

Grace: Oh – Maryland is in my mind – Maryland, Maryland – but I don't think it can be Maryland – it's just in my mind – Maryland – I don't know.

Maryland is sometimes referred to as 'the Catholic heartland of America'. There are numerous convents within the

state and many mother houses for orders such as the Sisters
of Mercy are in Maryland.

Bloxham: Can you tell me the names of some of the other
nuns?

Grace: Sister Benedicta, Sister Catherine, Sister Marguerite
who is still fat – still fat – Sister Marguerite who is so
kind to me.

Bloxham: Are there many nuns here?

Grace: About forty – everything seems to have changed –
everything has changed – people come more into the convent – people come – we always see more people – we
have – people now seem more in need of retreat than
ever before. (*Pause.*) I still want newspapers – I still want
books – I can hardly hold a book – not the big heavy
books they have here – my hands are so badly crippled –
but I still long for books and people to talk to and see –
talk to.

Bloxham: Have you seen your mother lately?

Grace: She has been once – yes – she is very old – very old
– I don't expect I'll see her again.

Bloxham: What did she tell you when she came to see you?

Grace: Not much. No. They're not supposed to tell us very
much. We didn't have long together and there was somebody else with us and my mother couldn't say much –
you get to a stage where you are so cut off from people
that you have nothing in common with people – that
sounds – hmm – that sounds peculiar. I had nothing to
talk to her about – I knew nobody now that she knows,
only people in close proximity to me in the convent – I
knew nobody else.

Bloxham: Had you many friends before you went into the
convent?

Grace: A few – yes – but they all – my mother said that
they married – they all married. (*Pause.*) A girl with a
funny name – uh a funny name – Luca – Lucilla?

Bloxham: What was her other name?

Grace: Lucilla – Carr – Carr I think – I can't remember – I can't remember what people are like now – it's so long since I had contact with people.

Bloxham: Were you great friends with Lucilla?

Grace: As friendly as girls of sixteen can be – we were friends one minute and not friends the next – and we argued and we had – petty little things – I suppose we were friends – she's the only one I can remember very well.

Bloxham: Had you any boyfriends at that age?

Grace: Oh no. I liked boys – I enjoyed their company – they liked me – I was a bit of a tomboy – but no special, particular boyfriend.

Bloxham: Do you know who the Pope is?

Grace: Oh yes – but I can't – we have a photograph – a picture of him, but I can't remember.

Bloxham: Has any special cardinal been to see you?

Grace: No. No. We laugh – we shouldn't laugh about it, but we laugh and say 'we are just the forgotten ones tucked away' – yes – poor Sisters of Mercy.

Bloxham: You are Sisters of Mercy are you?

Grace: We're supposed to be – I have my doubts sometimes – ah ah – well mercy – do people want mercy these days? Do people want charity? I don't think so.

That section made me wonder if Grace was indeed one of the Sisters of Mercy, whose mother convent is in Maryland. The editor of a Catholic newspaper in Des Moines pointed out to me, however, that the term 'sister of mercy' could be applied in a general way to any nun.

But even assuming that a nun would use the term in a precise way, the task of tracing her would still not be easy. For, after the Order was founded in America in 1843 from the parent house in Dublin, it grew prodigiously, and there were soon scores of independent convents all over the country. Eventually, in 1929, an effort was made at re-organisation, and a hundred and six separate units, each with its own reverend mother, formed a union – although another seventeen communities decided to stay independent.

Tracing Sister Grace could well take Sister Mary Felicitas another twenty-eight years!

> Bloxham: You don't have any girls' school attached to your convent?
>
> Grace: No. But the sisters sometimes go out and give religious instruction to schools – yes that's what I would – I can't go now of course – but I would love to have gone to see the children – to be with the children particularly. I think religious instruction is so dull – I would have them laughing – religion isn't meant to be staid and stuffy – it's meant to be funny. You're not meant to suffer religious instruction – it's meant to be fun – I would have made them enjoy it – yes – but I'm through – I can't go out – can't get about now – I'm just – sitting here (*self-rebukingly*) fount of infinite wisdom!
>
> Bloxham (*puzzled*): Fount of infinite wisdom?
>
> Grace (*laughing*): Ah – ho – yes.
>
> Bloxham: Do they treat you with great reverence?
>
> Grace: Oh no! Oh no! No. No. No reverence – but they like me and that's all I care.
>
> Bloxham: Perhaps you have a twinkle in your eye?
>
> Grace: I have a twinkle in both eyes – I think I have a sense of humour – perhaps which I shouldn't have – but people in the Bible had senses of humour.
>
> Bloxham: Have you still got the same Mother Superior?
>
> Grace: Yes. She's getting on but she seems to go on for ever – whereas – she hasn't been ill since I can remember – I wish I could be like her and get about.
>
> Bloxham: What does she say when she comes to see you?
>
> Grace: Oh she greets me and asks how I'm feeling – I usually say 'with my hands' which raises a chuckle. Yes – my gnarled hands – but she's very kind but aloof – cold – but I think basically very kind.
>
> Bloxham: Are there any that you have fun with?

Grace: There are a lot of younger ones coming now – the older ones have gone and there aren't many of us left who were here when I first came.

Bloxham: When you say 'gone', do you mean died?

Grace: Yes. Some of them have died – there was talk of closing down the convent – closing down the convent – put us all in one big convent farther away – I didn't hear much about it. They think I'm too semi-senile now to bother – I don't get told very much.

Bloxham: Would you like to go to a bigger place?

Grace: I would have liked to go to a bigger place, but now I think I'm gradually getting stiffer and stiffer and more and more creaky – that I would now like to stay where I am – I would now like to stay where I am.

Bloxham: Now this is a bit later – what have you heard about the war?

Grace: The war is over – one of the sisters said that it was terrible – they had dreadful gases and dreadful bombs – and – oh terrible, she said – terrible and they had seen photographs of awful things – of battles – and Germany lost the war – Germany didn't win.

Bloxham: Have you heard anything else?

Grace: No.

Bloxham: Do you have news from Italy?

Grace: There is news but I – I can't be bothered to listen to it.

Bloxham: How old are you now?

Grace: Sixty – sixties – very crippled – terrible pain – terrible pain in my stomach. It seems to be eating me away – I try and smile and laugh but it's a terrible pain – terrible pain.

Bloxham's subject was in so much discomfort that the hypnotist woke her up and ended the regression.

Chapter 11

THE FIGHT OF HMS *AGGIE*

THERE are other Bloxham tapes just as striking as the regressions of Jane Evans. The 'HMS *Aggie*' regression – a 'pressed' sailor aboard a British frigate two centuries ago, telling of a fight with a French ship off Calais – is as powerful and bloodcurdling as any dramatic work I have ever heard.

The swearing, illiterate gunner's mate, with his hacking cough and earthy chuckle, is as far removed as it is possible to imagine from the man under hypnosis, Graham Huxtable, a charming and soft spoken Swansea man. The voices of the two are not recognisably of the same person – the mate has a much deeper tone and a strong South-of-England country accent.

The mate uses archaic naval slang and speaks of practices aboard ship equally out of date. Parts of the tape were unintelligible to me until explained by historians at the National Maritime Museum at Greenwich. And the appalling picture of life aboard a ship such as the *Aggie*, verified by experts, removed for ever any lingering nostalgia I might have felt for the 'hearts of oak and jolly tars' traditions of the Royal Navy. As Silliman wrote in his journal of 1806: 'One particular class of men seems to be abandoned by society and relinquished to perpetual imprisonment and a slavery which, though honourable, cuts them off from most things which men hold dear.'

A modern historian, Mr Oliver Warner, asked to research the tape by Earl Mountbatten, former First Lord of the Admiralty, told me he was convinced of the authenticity of the tape 'simply by the reality of the conditions described, the man's general attitude and as much by his overall ignorance as by any facts of history he appears to be familiar with.'

This tape has to be heard to be fully appreciated and it was this experience which prompted Earl Mountbatten and his nephew, Prince Philip, to call in some Admiralty historians. Several ships' captains and ships have been suggested as possibly matching the captain of the *Aggie* and his vessel, but no one can specifically identify the action off the French coast. This is hardly surprising, for in a century full of blockades of French ports, chancing upon this one minor incident is truly expecting to find the needle in the naval haystack. Perhaps this published version will lead some researcher to have better luck than we have had so far.

As for Graham Huxtable, he is quite at a loss to explain the whole experience. He does not believe in reincarnation, but now wonders whether some theory of inherited memory might be an explanation. He speculates that because his ancestors came from Devon, they were perhaps associated with the sea.

Huxtable himself has never been to sea, served in the navy, nor had any interest in the topic. His wartime service was in the army and his involvement with tanks and never with ships.

The *Aggie* was his only regression. He met Bloxham in 1965, when accompanying someone going to the hypnotherapist for treatment and agreed to be one of the hypnotist's 'guinea pigs'. The climax, as the mate's leg is apparently shot away by cannon fire, was so agonising that the hypnotist had some difficulty in bringing Huxtable out of the trance. The hypnotist never asked him to do another tape.

Yet it had begun serenely enough, with the dialogue gradually growing in confidence, and punctuated by a strange, almost consumptive, deep cough which clearly does not belong to Huxtable. The mate finds himself aboard a 'rolling ship'.

Bloxham: What kind of ship is she?
Huxtable: Aaaah. (*Pause.*) Hell!
Bloxham: What kind of ship?
Huxtable: Always rolling.

Bloxham: Is she in a bad sea?
Huxtable: Aye – the sea's heavy (*bout of coughing*).
Bloxham: What is the name of this ship?
Huxtable: Call her *Aggie*.
Bloxham: What's her full name?
Huxtable: Fancy name. *Aggie, Aggus* . . . (*voice dies away muttering*).
Bloxham: Never mind, you'll remember shortly. Who is in command?
Huxtable: The cap'n.
Bloxham: Captain who?
Huxtable: Pearce. Cap'n Pearce.

There were close on twenty captains named Pearce or Pearse or Pearson, serving in the navy in the eighteenth century, so this information helped little in identifying the *Aggie*.

Bloxham: What sort of man is he?
Huxtable: He's fond of the cat?
Bloxham: Fond of the cat is he?
Huxtable: Aye, too fond!

The cat-o'-nine-tails, a whip with nine lashes, was the standard method of discipline in the British navy. A court martial offence could mean three hundred lashes, sometimes fatal, and a minor misdemeanour would merit six or a dozen across the bare back.

Bloxham: What are you in this ship?
Huxtable: Guns.
Bloxham: How are you dressed?
Huxtable (*pause*): 'Tarn' breeks (probably 'torn' breeches or trousers).
Bloxham: Breeks, yes?
Huxtable: Breeks and canvas shirt (quite typical for sailors of this period).
Bloxham: Canvas shirt?

Huxtable: Aye – yes – rough.

Bloxham: What are you like to look at? Dark or fair?

Huxtable: Dirty!

Bloxham: What do they call you?

Huxtable: Mate.

Bloxham: Are you the 'mate' or do you mean they call you 'mate'?

Huxtable: Gunner's mate . . . gunner's mate, that's me.

Bloxham: How many guns?

Huxtable (*with pride*): Ah, we've got some guns.

Bloxham: How many?

Huxtable: Sixteen a side. Aye, good guns.

A full battleship such as the *Victory* had a hundred guns, but the more mobile fighting ships, the frigates, had over thirty, counting stern guns and others. Huxtable is accurate, for as G. J. Marcus says of the eighteenth century in his naval history – 'there was a numerous class of thirty-two-gun frigates.'

Bloxham: Have you been in any battle?

Huxtable (*belligerently*): Where do you think I got these marks?

Bloxham: You what? (*unable to comprehend immediately that he is expected to see his subject as scarred*).

Huxtable: Where do you think I got these marks? (*Pause.*) I been in a fight – one or two.

Bloxham: Who did you fight?

Huxtable: Bloody Frogs!

Bloxham: Frogs, did you?

Huxtable: Aye, Frenchies. (*Pause.*) Bastards!

Bloxham: Did you sink the ship?

Huxtable: Aye, we had 'em.

Bloxham: What was the Frenchy's name? Did you know their ship?

Huxtable: Aye, they've got fancier names than we have. (*Pause.*) Don't know – didn't see her name.

Bloxham: Did you send her to the bottom?

Huxtable: Aye, with all hands . . . off their coast – we were their side – we were their side. They came out and they didn't come far!

Bloxham: What port was that?

Huxtable (*braggingly*): Any port – we done it – we done it before.

Bloxham: Were you lying in wait?

Huxtable: Aye – patrolling. Up and down – all we've done for months – patrol, patrol, patrol – got to keep 'em in, that's what the bosun says.

Blockades of the French coast were numerous and so were sinkings. The 'bosun' or boatswain was an officer responsible for crew discipline, amongst his other duties.

Bloxham: Have you taken part in any big battle?

Huxtable: We've fought 'em – we fought 'em. Always fighting 'em.

Bloxham: What is your name?

Huxtable: Don't have names on ships.

Bloxham: What was your name before you came aboard?

Huxtable: When I were a boy – Ben.

Bloxham: You can remember your name and your father's name can't you?

Huxtable: His name were Ben.

Bloxham: What was your father like to look at?

Huxtable: He were a thin man – thin man; he were tall, tall, thin man – not like me.

Bloxham: Are you short, short and fat?

Huxtable: Not fat! Not fat on this ship!

Bloxham: Is she badly found?

Huxtable: Don't get fat on weevils . . . worms and weevils and worms. Worms in the water tank too.

Bloxham: Did you have hard tack?

Huxtable: Tack? Tack? It's no bread.

Bloxham: What sort of bread was it?

Huxtable: Bread! They calls it bread. It's not bread – no –
takes yer teeth down!

The provisioning of ships was usually appalling during the
eighteenth century. Worms were commonplace in food and
water. As an example of what seamen were expected to eat,
a contemporary writer quoted by Sir William Laird Clowes in
his *The Royal Navy – a History*, said: 'Seamen in the king's
ships have made buttons for their jackets and trowsers with
the cheese they were served with, having preferred it, by
reason of its tough and durable quality, to buttons made of
common metal.'

Bloxham: Were there many casualties when you engaged
the French ship?
Huxtable: Sank it!
Bloxham: Yes, but did any of your men get hurt?
Huxtable: Hurt, aye, hurt . . . splinters.

Splinters were a main hazard in actions between the wooden
warships of the time.

Bloxham: Splinters? Did they carry the masts away or
something?
Huxtable: No, no. We held our sticks (masts) . . . it's when
the shot comes in – aye – splinters fly.
Bloxham: How much canvas do you carry?
Huxtable: Enough. More than the Frog.
Bloxham: How many officers have you aboard?
Huxtable (*disgusted*): Officers, hah! They call themselves
sailors. . . . Pearce is a sailor – a bastard – but he knows
the sea. He's a sailor.
Bloxham: Have you sailed with him before?
Huxtable: I've never sailed with anyone else . . . I've been
here since they. . . . (*voice fades away.*)
Bloxham: What's Captain Pearce like?
Huxtable (*explosively*): Bastard!

Bloxham: Is he a rough looking man?

Huxtable: Hah. He washes!

Bloxham: What sort of clothes does he wear?

Huxtable: Like officers – britches, shoon, buckles.

Bloxham: Does he wear a wig?

Huxtable: Aye, he isn't tarred and greased like we are.

Bloxham: What sort of hat does he wear?

Huxtable (*pause*): Points.

Bloxham: A pointed one – how many points?

Huxtable: Two points sideways . . . sideways – 'thwart-ships (*begins to chuckle*) – hat's on 'thwart-ships – I couldn't tell 'im that – he'd 'ave my back!

Bloxham: Has he ever had you thrashed?

Huxtable: No, not me . . . no, I can lay a gun. Aye, I can lay the sixteen of 'em, aye.

As with the ordinary sailors, the description of the officers rings true. Officers' dress was not regularised until 1825, but knee breeches, shoes, buckles and wigs were all in fashion. 'Shoon' is archaic, and "thwart-ships' was indecipherable to me initially. It's a naval term meaning 'sideways on', and the two-pointed cocked hat often worn by captains was sometimes worn sideways by the more eccentric masters, which probably accounted for the mate's laughter. This is clear in an account written in the nineteenth century, also quoted by Clowes:

'The cocked hat had previously been worn as individual fancy suggested, but in 1825 it was so prescribed as to be wearable "fore and aft" only, although, until some years later, a few perverse officers continued to have their hats so made that they could be worn athwart-ships.'

Bloxham: Which port did you leave?

Huxtable: Months ago . . . (*bout of deep coughing*). This bloody sea!

Bloxham: Have you got a wife?

Huxtable: Wife? Wife? Sailors? No, sailors don't 'ave wives – women! When we can get 'em . . . when they lets 'em on . . . high jinks then, when they do . . . catch one. Hah, hah.

Bloxham: Catch one, do you?

Huxtable: Some, some. They're all right . . . for what they are, they'll do. A man's too long afloat and they don't let us off.

Bloxham: They don't let you off?

Huxtable: Not them that's been pressed.

Bloxham: Oh, you were pressed were you?

Huxtable: Aye, pressed, but a serving man now – I'll stay. I can lay a gun.

The 'press' gangs were notorious in the eighteenth century and by law they could 'impress' any able-bodied man with experience of the sea between the ages of eighteen and fifty-five. In practice, they took anyone, sometimes penetrating miles inland if the need to crew a ship was great enough. In 1770 only one-fifth of Britain's sailors were 'volunteers', and the historian J. R. Hutchinson wrote: 'At times it was unsafe for any able-bodied man to venture abroad unless he had on him an undeniable protection or wore a dress that unmistakably proclaimed the gentleman.'

Even the founder of the Methodist Church, John Wesley, was once a victim of a press gang in that century! And once aboard ship, there was no getting off when the ship was in port. Women were taken in 'bumboats' to naval ships in harbour and were allowed aboard for the benefit of the ordinary seamen. Officers were not allowed to bring their 'ladies' aboard, but then they were allowed to go ashore!

Bloxham: Which is your favourite port?

Huxtable: Ports are all the same – taverns and bumboats and stinks.

Bloxham: Does your ship stink?

Huxtable: Aye, to the wood she stinks.

Bloxham: What?

Huxtable: Come up windward of her and you're all right.

But she stinks to the wood . . . fair enough, all ships stink.

Bloxham: Can you tell me the names of the other officers?

Huxtable: Pearce, Captain Pearce. He's a sailor.

Bloxham: Is it Pearce or Piers?

Huxtable: Aye.

Bloxham: Can you tell me the name of your ship, the *Aggie*?

Huxtable: Aye, it's writ up front.

Bloxham: It is? Can you read it?

Huxtable: Me! (*Laughs.*) How should I read? I got no learnin'.

Bloxham: What?

Huxtable: How should I read, I got no learnin'.

Bloxham: No? Do you think this ship is called the *Agamemnon*?

Huxtable: Aye – could be – could be. *Aggie* we call 'er . . . (*aggressively*) *Aggie, Aggie*, you rolling bitch!

Bloxham: What year is this? (*Long silence.*) Have there been any special happenings in the last year or two – battles that you've heard of, or wars?

Huxtable: Wars? There's always wars now. We're at war now. We're fighting – French. Aye.

Bloxham: Who is the monarch, who is king?

Huxtable: King, king! Him!

Bloxham: King of England, do you know?

Huxtable (*rolling words contemptuously*): German George.

Bloxham: Did you ever see him?

Huxtable: No.

For over a century, from 1714 until 1820, all the kings of England were called George and might have been referred to mockingly and for various reasons as 'German George'.

George I was a German, the Elector of Hanover, invited to take the throne in 1714, and he was disliked partly because he refused to learn to speak English. Apparently he had a disastrous initiation into the language when he was coached to say

on arrival 'I have come for the good of you all'. It is alleged
he mistakenly, but fairly accurately, said 'I have come for all
of your goods.'

Under George I, the Channel was patrolled in 1715 against
the French, for fear that they would support the Jacobite rising
to put a Stuart king back on the English throne.

George II was born in Germany and was never popular with
the English – his favourite pastime was counting his wealth,
coin by coin! The coast of France was blockaded again from
1745, when the Stuarts attempted to put the 'Young Pretender'
on the throne. There was more action in the Channel and
French invasion barges were again poised from 1756, during
the Seven Years War. And from 1759, Admiral Hawke initiated
the 'closed' blockade of French ports, with French vessels being attacked at their harbour mouths.

George III was crowned in 1760 and was both King of
England and King of Hanover. He was not popular in the first
part of his reign, and his bouts of insanity and mismanage-
ment of the American War of Independence did not make him
more so. During the Napoleonic wars, from 1803 until 1814,
there was a virtually non-stop closed blockade of French
ports.

Bloxham: Have you seen any important people at any time,
who have visited your ship?

Huxtable: Everybody's important who comes in a barge –
(*in a strong voice mimics orders aboard ship*). – 'Man the
sides, man the rigging – ah, barge alongside – blow bosun
– pipe, pipe 'em up the ladder – stand to the guns – stand
to the guns – man the yards – dress the rigging' (*last
word almost inaudible, and the mate resumes in his
normal voice*). Never looks, never looks. Who cares? 'E
don't care when 'e comes.

Bloxham: He what?

Huxtable: Pearce – Pearce cares. When 'e comes, Pearce
cares! – the starter, the bosun's got 'is starter out on the
men then. Aye, he's free with 'is starter.

Bloxham: He's free with his what?

Huxtable (*angry*): 'E's free with 'is starter – too free with
'is starter – aah, I'd like to bend it round 'is back!

A 'starter' was a length of rope with a 'Turk's head' knot,
used by bosuns and bosuns' mates to enforce discipline. Its
use was banned in 1809.

Bloxham: Did they used to flog the men?

Huxtable (*angrily*): What do you mean 'used to flog 'em',
they flog 'em now!

Bloxham: They flog them now do they?

Huxtable (*opening words a whispered command*): 'Keep
your eyes down boy! Keep your eyes down! Keep 'em in
the boat!' – that's what I tell 'em. I learned.

Bloxham: You learned did you?

Huxtable: Aye. Keep yer eyes down and yer tongues still
boys! Hmmm. Cold, cold. (He appears to be shivering
and Bloxham puts a blanket over his body.)

Bloxham: How old were you when you first went to sea?

Huxtable: When I was took? Hmm.

Bloxham: Were you very young?

Huxtable: Aye, I was young – a lad.

Bloxham: Was your father a sailor?

Huxtable: Big Ben? No.

Bloxham: What did he do?

Huxtable: He carried wood to the tower . . . the tower on
the cliff.

Bloxham: What cliff was this?

Huxtable: A cliff, a cliff. . . . 'Sho'm', shore. . . .

Bloxham: What's the name of the place?

Huxtable: 'Sho'm', shore. . . .

Here and elsewhere, the mate mumbles a word which
sounds like 'Sho'm', but could well be a local pronounciation
of 'Shoreham', a village on the English coast in Sussex. 'Wood
for the tower' could refer to a beacon lit on a cliff in rough

weather to aid ships, a forerunner to the modern lighthouse;
or it could be part of the beacon system set up on the South
coast in the time of Napoleon to warn of a French invasion.

Bloxham: How did they catch you?

Huxtable: They chased me.

Bloxham: What were you doing at the time?

Huxtable: With old Moll.

Bloxham (*amusingly misunderstanding*): Oh, with a moll
were you?

Huxtable (*impatiently*): Old Moll, old Moll.

Bloxham: Who was she?

Huxtable: A mare! . . . Old Moll, aye, you couldn't keep 'er
in the furrow. (*Chuckles*) Old Moll she used to pull off all
the time.

Bloxham: Were you ploughing?

Huxtable: Ploughin' – saw 'em coming – they were at the
other end as well – they got me.

Bloxham: They got you, were you very distressed at the
time?

Huxtable (*moans*): It still hurts.

Bloxham: Your head?

Huxtable: That's how I got this! . . . Burning cold.

Bloxham: Were there many more men pressed into service?

Huxtable: Aye, gangs are always pressing . . . aye, they're
in the ports and inshore, the villages, they go miles inland, they take 'em. Where they find 'em they take 'em.
Huh! . . . I weren't drunk, I were ploughin'!

Bloxham: I expect your family wondered where you'd
gone?

Huxtable (*chuckling again*): Aye, they must have wondered where I'd gone. Aye, I wonder what's happened to
old Moll? She's standin' there now. That's a good year
or so.

Bloxham: Did your father have a farm?

Huxtable: No! He looked after the tower, he kept the fire
there, kept the wood on the top.

Bloxham: What was the nearest town to your house?
Huxtable: 'Sho'm'.
Bloxham: Your head's feeling better now?
Huxtable: Aye, that were a dint that were.
Bloxham: What is the most exciting battle you've been in?
Huxtable: Excitin'? (*Pause.*) Hmm – lads ask questions like
   that.
Bloxham: What do you usually tell them?
Huxtable: It's not excitin', lad . . . you'll be frightened.
Bloxham: You are frightened?
Huxtable (*sternly*): *They'll* be frightened – like I were.
   They'll learn, they'll learn.

The *Aggie* tape now approaches its climax. As if excited,
perhaps by the proximity of battle, Huxtable's voice becomes
louder and more confident. Sometimes, he describes what is
happening, at others he calls out his orders to the gun crews,
and sometimes he mimics orders he hears. The 'matches' referred to were lengths of rope soaked in tar and lit to provide
the spark by which the guns were fired. It has been thought
likely that sailors blew on the spark to keep it alight, but the
method described here of swinging the match seems more
sensible and likely. A watchful gunner's mate could quickly
see who was neglecting that vital spark, by watching the swing
of an arm.

'Jolly Guns', I took to be a reference to an officer named
Jolly, of whom there were several in the service.

Bloxham: Now this is a bit later. What are you doing?
Huxtable (*tensely*): Waiting! Always waiting!
Bloxham: Outside a French port?
Huxtable: They'll come out.
Bloxham: They'll come out, will they?
Huxtable (*rapping out orders, rising to a shout*): At the
   ready! Keep yer match ready boy – keep yer match ready
   – ah, cover it, you fool! Ah, these boys, these boys –
   swing it, swing it! Don't let that spark go out. Don't let

it go. Swing that . . . you won't get another – not until the firepots come out, and then you'll stay there.

Bloxham: You've got your guns trained have you?

Huxtable: The guns are trained! They're laid out, but they're waiting. They'll come, they'll come – they always come at first light.

Bloxham: Do you get plenty of sleep?

Huxtable: Sleeps when you can, where and when, when we're waiting.

Bloxham (an old sailor himself): Are you doing watch and watch?

Huxtable: Watch and stand-by, watch and stand-by – there's mist, mist.

Bloxham: Is mist your friend or your enemy?

Huxtable: It's good to stand-by in the mist and the shore batteries can't see us – we're in close – they can't see us. They might see the tops'l, they might, they might, but not until it's too late – I'll catch 'em as they clear the heads – we're waiting, waiting – three days, three days now, now – this mist'll lift.

Bloxham: Do you know what port you're waiting outside?

Huxtable: It is. (*Pause.*) Calais, Calais, Calais.

Bloxham: Have you come out of Dover?

Huxtable: Out of the Sound we came this time, out of the Sound.

Bloxham: Plymouth Sound?

Huxtable: Aye, we've been out a month, a month or more. (*Breaks off with Bloxham, to shout back an answer to some command he has heard.*) Aye aye, sir! Aye aye, ready sir! (*Softly.*) You bastard!

Bloxham: Who gave you the order? The captain?

Huxtable (*tersely*): The gunner.

Bloxham: The gunner?

Huxtable: Lieutenant.

Bloxham: Do you know his name?

Huxtable: Guns – Jolly Guns. (*Chuckles grimly.*) He's a jolly man I don't think!

Bloxham: You don't like him. Is he tough?

Huxtable: An officer doesn't have to be tough.

Bloxham: He doesn't have to be?

Huxtable (*ignoring Bloxham and shouting a command*): Swing that match boy, swing it – keep it alight!

Bloxham: Is your ship yawing a bit?

Huxtable: Ah, she's just holding, just holding, holding up against the wind – have to go about soon – in close – can hear the breakers now.

Bloxham: Can you? That's a bit too close.

Huxtable: Ah, we're close in. Ah, Pearce does this, he does this. He lays in close and waits.

Bloxham: It might be good navigation, but it's a bit tricky isn't it?

Huxtable (*softly*): Aye, they say 'e can smell the sand.

Bloxham: Do they?

Huxtable: They say 'e can smell it. (*Pause.*) Ah God, wish they'd come.

Bloxham: Now this is a bit later, is the enemy leaving his anchorage?

Huxtable: Third time about – he's still not coming – not much mist now! Not much mist now. We'll be clear – in five minutes we'll be clear. (*Breaks off again.*) Stand by! Stand by to go about! Stand by, you're going about. Aye aye, sir – now watch your, watch your chocks. Watch your chocks! Well done lad – good – swing that match – swing that match. (*Pause.*) Aye aye, sir – aye, aye, we're ready – keep your matches up boys – swing now – stand by – hold boy, hold, hold. Aye aye, sir. (*Pause.*) Chock up a bit on this one, chock up, gun her up! Watch that priming – bit more here – bit more – that's right. Now this one – bring her up – bring her up – bring her up on the chocks – up more – up, up – get your muzzle up – pin it up – that's right – steady now lad – steady now, steady, steady – all right lad? – you'll be all right now, just hold it! (*Voice becomes a bellow.*) Get from behind, number three – you fool – GET FROM BEHIND NUMBER

THREE – if that runs back on you, you'll have your legs off, aye!

Bloxham: Have you fired your cannon?

Huxtable: Waiting, waiting! Waiting for the order – steady lads, steady – now hold it, hold it hold it – wait for the order, wait for it – swing those matches, aye sirree – stand clear from behind – NOW you fool. Now up fool now – NOW! (*screams in exultation as the shot is fired*) – Well done lads – run 'em up, run 'em up, get 'em up, get 'em up – get 'em up the front – (*shrieks*) – pull that man out, pull 'im out – send him in the cockpit – now get 'im back – get up there – get on the chocks there – run them up again!

The shot in – ramrods – swab it, swab it, you fool, swab it first – the shot in, shot in – come on number four, you should be up by now – shot in, ram it home – prime – swing those matches – aye, aye, sir – ready!

And again lads – you had him then – hurry men – by God you bastard – got him that aim – that's the way to lay a gun – My Christ, they've got old Pearce, they've got Pearce – (*sudden terrible screaming*) – MY BLOODY LEG – (*screaming and moaning uncontrollably*) – MY LEG – MY LEG!

With some difficulty, Bloxham, who appears to be slapping Huxtable's face, manages to bring him out of the trance and reassures him that his leg is still in one piece. Both men are clearly shaken by the experience.

The *Aggie* is certainly the most dramatic tape in Bloxham's collection. The gunner's mate, with every word he utters, his coughing and cursing, reeks of the sea and his own time. He has a credible personality, displayed in chuckling affection for his lost youth as a ploughboy with 'old Moll', to his sour acceptance of life at sea. His pride in being able to 'lay a gun' is well founded, as experts who have heard the tape have verified.

But did such an incident ever happen? Was there ever an

action off Calais in the reign of a 'German George' involving a British frigate skippered by a 'Captain Pearce'?

The problem is that we don't know the full 'fancy name' of the *Aggie*. And there are listed numerous sea captains at war against the French named Pearce, Pearse, Pierce, Pearson, Piercy, Peard, etc. Even could we identify the captain concerned, we would not necessarily be much the wiser, for the naval historian Sir William Laird Clowes in his comprehensive history of the service tells us that: 'Until 1814 there was, using terms in their modern sense, no official navy list. For many years previously, there had been published, at intervals, lists of flag officers . . . they showed merely the seniority and dates of commissions and gave no other information whatsoever.'

Unless the incident off Calais was a major skirmish worthy of being recorded and possibly published in London at the time, it is unlikely the ship will ever be traced, although there were undoubtedly numerous actions such as the one described by the gunner's mate. There must in particular have been many such outside Calais spread over the ten years from 1803, when Napoleon in the reign of George III placed twenty-seven thousand troops and four hundred invasion barges in Calais, Dunkirk and Ostend. The coastline 'bristled with cannon', and up to a hundred and fifty British ships are estimated to have assisted in the blockade.

The historian Captain A. T. Mahon refers to just one phase of this protracted action when he writes: 'In the end, they [French troops in Calais] were also moved to the Boulogne coast, and their boats, after some sharp fighting with British cruisers, joined the main flotilla in the four channel ports.'

Was the *Aggie* one of the British cruisers in this 'sharp fighting', or is she a frigate from one of the several blockades of the previous century? Did she exist at all, outside the imagination of Graham Huxtable? Regrettably, we may never know.

Chapter 12

THE SPY ON THE CLIFF

OF the remaining Bloxham tapes, most contained little drama and less history. There were no reincarnated Caesars or Napoleons on the couch in Bloxham's consulting room, and if his hypnotised people were borrowing their stories from the pages of history, they modestly refrained from giving themselves the leading roles. They mostly regressed to become ordinary people, bystanders whose careers never added a penny to any historian's bill for stationery or midnight oil.

They were usually more impressive in the twentieth century – a fair cross-section of teachers, engineers, civil servants, housewives and journalists. But mostly the events they described were untraceable today.

Sometimes they seemed so vague or blankly ignorant of events on a wider scale in the time they were describing, that I found myself muttering in exasperation – 'but they ought to know that!' I was forgetting that ours is the first century to be saturated with newspaper, radio and television coverage and to take for granted travel and the average man's literacy and nodding acquaintance with world affairs. The people in the regressions were entitled to their ignorance, but it didn't assist my researches.

Occasionally, their routine of work and family concerns was broken by a single event, and for a moment the regression could be measured for accuracy against the history books. My friend John Pike, who under hypnosis witnessed the execution of King Charles I, was typical of those who in a humdrum life described one extraordinary incident verifiable today.

But the questioning established only a few facts – that the

king was a small man and wore a white shirt (some reference books say he wore two to keep out the cold!); and that on the platform, along with the soldiers and the executioner, was a bishop – in reality the Bishop of London.

Historically this is disappointing and does not help establish whether the regression is fantasy or 'memory'. Ironically, the detail is so scant that it's almost a typically genuine eye-witness account! John Pike remembers chiefly his sense of pity for the king and his shock at what was unfolding before his eyes. The average man, watching an event as emotionally charged as a public execution, would probably recall it as a similar series of impressions, visual and emotional, and not in the dry and detailed way of the historian or the journalist.

Elsewhere in the regression, John Pike casually mentions one or two names which are known to history, but as an 'ordinary man' he doesn't know very much about them! He had heard of George Villiers, a man so unpopular in England, say the history books, that his friendship with the king was one of the underlying causes of the civil war – King Charles thought so highly of Villiers that a wit, watching Villiers ride by, observed: 'all the king's council sits on one horse.'

But John Pike had clearly not read that history book, nor in his regression personality was he familiar with that sort of gossip. Yet I suspect he knew just as much as might be expected of the son of a seventeenth-century Worcestershire farmer.

Other regressions have even less to offer the researcher – memorable perhaps only for an item of gossip or a rumour. A woman who claimed to live in the reign of Queen Elizabeth I had heard that all the queen's Maids of Honour, in their anxiety to catch husbands, had become pregnant at the same time, and that sharp-tongued Queen Bess had then decided it would be more appropriate in future to call them 'Ladies in Waiting'!

Even an anecdote of that sort can be historically tested. It is a fact that, at the Elizabethan court, a Maid of Honour seeking a noble marriage, would happily get pregnant by an earl and then ask the queen to have a word with the gentleman concerned. Many noblemen, including Sir Walter Raleigh, were trapped into marriage in this way. One earl, who refused the queen's advice to transform a pregnant Maid of Honour into a countess, was banished from court!

The difficulty of assessing fairly some of the information given in a regression is sometimes more extreme because the accepted historical record of the times is either blank or frankly unreliable. As Bloxham said, some historians 'wrote with a political pen' and their work is not to be trusted. More frequently, the area is simply a gap in the history books. A regression to Ancient Greece, which described a battle in Thrace, between Greeks and Turks, was not worth researching because the text books have so little to offer.

If society ever accepted the notion that people under hypnosis could be regressed to have reliable knowledge of other times, the study of history would be revolutionised!

Serious historians are fully aware of the limitations of their craft. As they assessed many of the Bloxham Tapes, I noted that they were as much concerned with 'the feel' of the narrative – an accumulation of minor social detail suggesting the person had a real sense of what it would be like to live in those times – as they were with checking off any list of names or facts.

My view too is that for a tape to be credible in any worthwhile sense, it should be historically verifiable and convey a real sense of the period. Most tapes were not worth investigating in detail because, even if corroborated, they would be unremarkable and could adequately be explained as 'historical fantasy'.

Of the handful of tapes I chose to research in any depth, there is only one we have not analysed so far – 'the spy on the cliff'. In some ways, this regression is the most fascinating of all the tapes. It is one of my favourites, but I regard it also as a comparative failure. Even after careful investigation, it has too many question marks against it for me to be able to say: this is so remarkable it must be more than a 'historical fantasy'.

Yet this regression has a great air of reality, there is a real knowledge of dress, local geography and of the period, and the central character is droll and entertaining. He knows some fascinating things and the reader may find him more convincing than I do. My instinct is to put him on one side, with the woman who thought she was Queen Elizabeth I, and say: 'this may be a historical fantasy, but it doesn't mean that the others are equally suspect.'

But the 'spy on the cliff' is an attractive rascal and his story makes excellent reading. He is one of nature's outsiders, a dry stick of a man, who three centuries ago earned his living as a spy, informing on smugglers and getting them hanged.

During a two-hour regression, this seventeenth-century undercover agent convincingly aged from a somewhat insecure loner, with a mild conscience about his work and the makings of a drink problem, to become a morose and rheumaticky old man, settled in life, haunted by his past, and still with a drink problem.

If the quantity surveyor from the north of England, who regressed to become this lonely man, could write dialogue the way he speaks it under hypnosis, he might have a future as a writer of fiction.

The opening is hesitant and uncertain, as if the hypnotised man can scarcely believe the new information in his mind. He suggests that his name might be Arthur Sankey, his father perhaps once kept a store in the Cornish village of Mevagissey, and the King of England might be 'Charles something-or other'.

He is in no doubt about what he can see – it is a moonlit night on a clifftop near the Devonshire village of Clovelly.

> Sankey: I carry a cutlass – I am dressed in blue breeches, blue jacket with a cue to my hair (the ends tied at the nape of the neck) – I am looking for a ship from the cliffs.
> Bloxham: Are you a customs man?
> Sankey: I think I must be – though I have no hat – only my suit of blue and a cutlass.

Sankey is after smugglers and tells Bloxham he believes his headquarters might be in Clovelly. He gives an accurate description of the village – 'a small blue bay with a quayside facing the town, very steep streets, cobbled and narrow.' – But soon he sees a ship from the clifftop.

Bloxham: Are they showing a light?

Sankey: No. No. They are being walked in – two boats I can see.

Bloxham: What is 'walked in'?

Sankey: They must come in so slowly – a boat without the power of sail – come in so slowly so as not to damage herself or rouse suspicion with the rattle of block and tackle and shouting of the bosun – they put a crew in two small boats – tie rags round the oars to muffle the sound – pass a line from the stem of the ship to each boat and slowly tow her in very gently (*pause*) there is a man standing in one of the small boats – I think I know the man as Croker – he is standing in the bow of the nearest small boat making signals with his arms, gently like a bird flapping his wings.

Bloxham: What do the signals mean?

Sankey: Keep it steady boys, forward and steady – very steady.

Bloxham: Have you ever arrested Croker?

Sankey: No. No.

Bloxham: But you think you might get him now?

Sankey: I am alone – I have no comrades – I am only watching. One boat is losing way on the big ship – now she's right again – she's beginning to swing.

The smugglers land quietly on the beach and Sankey notes that Croker is wearing a tricorne hat. But he is more struck by the dress of another man from the ship, whom he decides, sarcastically, is 'French' –

Sankey: Lace at the cuffs – but that coat was never made to

meet and button at the front – the edges are just looped
together with braid – his hat is side-to-side not front-to-
back – he looks like a doll with a handle on each side of
his head!

Sankey makes no attempt to catch the smugglers. He is
content to watch, and pays particular attention to a cave
where the contraband is taken initially. Slowly and drily, he
speaks of the smuggling trade.

Sankey: They all seem to have the same idea – a deserted
    beach or cave – usually an outlet to an inn or large
    house – or, as I have heard, to a church.
Bloxham: Have you had an instance of smugglers using a
    church?
Sankey: Not to my experience. But as I say I have heard of
    it – (instances of smuggled goods stored in church towers
    are recorded) – they all make the same mistake of think-
    ing if the coast is uninhabited then it is deserted – but
    it is never so – sooner or later someone will remark upon
    peculiar visits of boats or men – or find trinkets dropped
    in the sand for no apparent reason.
Bloxham: Have you found trinkets?
Sankey: I have found gold coins – silver coins – French
    coins mainly. There is a flourishing trade between the
    Cornish coast and France.
Bloxham: What do they smuggle?
Sankey: Many things – they smuggle brandy, lace and I be-
    lieve some sweet-scented fatty stuff.
Bloxham: What do they use this for?
Sankey: Washing – I don't know what they call it, but it's
    like our tallow soap or supposed to be.

In the seventeenth and eighteenth centuries, highly taxed
luxury goods like brandy and lace, both made in France, were
stock-in-trade for English smugglers. So too were the fashion-

able perfumed soaps and pomades developed in Paris in the seventeenth century.

The grim battle of wits between smugglers and customs men had already been going on for centuries. The writer Geoffrey Chaucer was one of the best known early customs officers back in the fourteenth century. Up to 1688, 'tunnage and poundage' meant that the crown imposed a duty of two shillings a cask on imported wine and two-and-a-half percent duty on everything else. Additional forms of duties were also levied. Consequently, the smugglers, or free traders, carried on their daring traffic all along the south coast, and became even more active and highly organised when taxes were increased on imports in 1688.

There was a massive loss of revenue to the state, and apart from severe penalties – hanging and transportation – one attempted remedy was the introduction of 'ryding officers'. Arthur Sankey could well have been one of these – for a 'ryding officer' is described as 'an official appointed for sections of the coast, who will observe from clifftops and try to arrange for the taking of smugglers'.

It was dangerous work. Customs officials were sometimes murdered or brutally assaulted – one was staked out on a beach to drown in the incoming tide and another had his nose cut off, presumably as a warning to mind his own business. Sometimes they were kidnapped and taken across to France on the smugglers' ship. If they were lucky they were perhaps simply tied up while the smugglers unloaded their cargoes, and were set free afterwards. In parts of the country, communities went in fear of the free traders who seemed often above the law.

But 'ryding officers' were a better known feature of the eighteenth than the seventeenth century, and my unease with the Sankey regression was the growing feeling that he had named 'Charles' as king, when perhaps he should have said 'George'. The Stuart kings were exclusively seventeenth-century whilst the Georges were eighteenth – the period when smuggling reached its bloodthirsty peak.

For one thing, Sankey made no mention of smuggling of exports out of England, which in the seventeenth century was as profitable as anything else. Wool was the great cargo for free traders, who were so active that death was the penalty for its illegal export.

Wool so dominated commercial thinking in the seventeenth century that in 1666 Parliament passed a 'Burial in Woollens Act', which meant that, after every funeral, two witnesses had to swear before a notary that 'the corps was nott put in, wrapt or wound up or buried in any shirt, shift, sheet or shroude made or mingled with flaxe, hempe, silk, haire, gold or silver or other than what is made of sheep's wool only.'

Bloxham: Have you ever had to do battle with smugglers?
Sankey: Oh, yes. They are all pretty much of the same ilk. They are tough but frightened. I seem to have a memory of going into an unlighted room with several others and there was a fight. I think my left arm was given a blow. I don't think with any weapon but with a club. It seems to ache now and again.
Bloxham: Have you ever had to kill one of them?
Sankey: When I have to fight a man I try not to kill him with my cutlass – he is useless to the magistrate then.
Bloxham: Are you taught swordplay?
Sankey: I was not taught it – but partly for my swordplay I follow this calling – the rapier is too finicky – only one point – with the cutlass you have cut and thrust – it is heavy bladed but merciful – used properly you can lay a person senseless rather than kill or mutilate him.
Bloxham: Have you ever been seriously wounded?
Sankey: No. Only twice have I ever faced a really good steelman amongst smugglers. Both used rapiers. One rapier against another and the better swordsman usually wins – but I had an edge to use as well as a point – if you sweep downwards with the curve of the cutlass, you can dash the rapier from his hand. In France I believe they say you should 'hold a rapier lightly like a bird – too loosely and

it flies away – too tightly and it suffocates'. It was quite easy to dash it from his hand with a left downwards movement with the back of the sword – taking it just below the guard with a return parry to the left.

Fencing is certainly a subject Arthur Sankey seems to know something about, although modern enthusiasts would debate his preference for the cutlass. They favour the speed of the lighter rapier. An expert on the subject told me he had heard the saying 'a rapier is like a bird etc.'. He was told it by the coach to a French Olympic team, and he understood it was a centuries-old maxim from France!

Sankey next gives a fairly accurate picture of the life of a 'ryding officer'.

Bloxham: What happened to this man?
Sankey: He was taken before the magistrates – I believe he
    was hanged – I left before it happened.
Bloxham: Do they ever try to bribe you?
Sankey: They never know I'm there.
Bloxham: How do you get them into custody?
Sankey: I study them and catch them when they least
    expect it – the king's men take them.
Bloxham: Are you one of the king's men?
Sankey: I am not an officer with the king's men.
Bloxham: Are you an excise man?
Sankey: Yes and no. I do not ride from village to village
    demanding dues I think have not been paid – I do not
    wear a blue uniform or hat. They stand before someone
    and say 'I arrest you in the name of the king' – and they
    are promptly disembowelled.
Bloxham: Do you enjoy your job?
Sankey: Sometimes – up to the point where the poor beasts
    are taken – then I go back to the inn and pack to leave.
    Then in some secluded inn between there and my next
    stopping place, I try to forget what those poor beasts are
    about to suffer – I drink to forget.

Bloxham: Do you know this inn well?

Sankey: The Red Savage Inn – called I believe after some savages supposed to live across the ocean – it seems a strange colour for a man. This is Clovelly – it is very pretty but I seem fated to be allowed no rest – I travel – I obtain the evidence for arrests – these are the responsibilities of my duties – I merely discover 'why, what and who' and the king's men do the rest.

Bloxham: What happens if they get caught?

Sankey: All convicted of smuggling are hanged – all I have caught are hanged – but I am never called to witness. It's a hard thing to live with – condemning a man to death – I try not to think about it – I try not to remember them – an executioner's life is a hard one, he finds difficulty in living with himself unless he is not quite right in the head – I feel the same way although I do not execute them.

Bloxham: Do you know the executioner?

Sankey: I do not know the executioner – there's a different one in each town.

Bloxham: Is there any appeal?

Sankey: No. Execution is summary within the parish.

Bloxham: Have you seen men hanged?

Sankey: No – only by accident. I have seen the results hanging in chains on the gallows – having been hanged hours earlier – the big black birds, crows and rooks, perch on the shoulders waiting to be sure the eyes are ready for eating.

Bloxham: How long do they leave them in chains?

Sankey: Until the bones fall apart – you smell an execution for a mile away – it is an example – the stink is terrible.

The practice of hanging in chains became common in the eighteenth century, and was known as 'gibbeting'. Highwaymen, pirates and smugglers were usually the victims – highwaymen were exhibited in chains at the roadsides where they had practised their trade. There was usually a pirate on view at the execution dock at Wapping as a warning to sailors, and in the smuggler's home village a miscreant might be on display as 'a dreadful memento to youth, how they swerve from the paths of rectitude and transgress the laws of their country'.

It was a grisly business but, as Sankey said, the victim had been 'hanged hours earlier'. When dead he was taken down and put in chains – the idea was to hold the body together as long as possible as an example to the community.

The process is described by F. F. Nicholls in his book *Honest Thieves – the violent heyday of English smuggling*: 'After removal from the gallows, the body was soused in tar to make it more weatherproof, and an elaborate network of chains or metal straps was measured to fit the body like a bespoke suit, and was fitted to hold the limbs together when decay occurred.

'Then the whole contraption was suspended by more chains from a strong wooden frame, the gibbet, which was usually erected in a high place. These gibbets and their ghastly burdens became a part of the century's folklore, and are often casually referred to in the literature of the period. There was a strong local tradition that the highwayman John Whitfield was gibbeted alive by the roadside near Weatherall, Carlisle, and that he hung for days in agony until mercifully shot by a passing stage coach guard. It was said that a robin nested in the empty skull of Tom Otter of Lincoln.'

Little wonder that Arthur Sankey seemed to view gibbeting with some horror, and most smugglers shared his sentiments! One noted cut-throat had such a dread of being gibbeted that he died soon after he was measured for his suit of chains, well in advance of the execution. Others were made of sterner stuff – some of the notorious Hawkhurst gang of smugglers were sentenced to be gibbeted, others to be hanged. Before the executions, one of the gang sympathised with Fairall, a ringleader who was to be gibbeted. Fairall smiled at him and replied calmly: 'We shall be hanging in the sweet air, when you are rotting in your grave!'

Bloxham: What did you do before?

Sankey: Five or six years ago I wandered about the country-side getting into scrapes and out of them.

Bloxham: What sort of scrapes?

Sankey: Oh, all sorts – over women, money or just plain drunk.

Bloxham: Were you fond of ale?

Sankey: I used to like to converse with people in the inns – I think I was taught the beginnings of swordsmanship with an old sea dog in Mevagissey.

Bloxham: Was he an interesting character?

Sankey: He was blunt, dark and dirty but one of the better kinds that go to sea. He had lost three fingers off his left hand – the little finger and the two next to it. And his dexterity with a cutlass was amazing to see. At forty-eight years he was getting to be an old man. He taught me – it is a heavy weapon but he had thick, strong wrists.
I practised – he used to thump me across the buttocks with the flat of the blade if I did something wrong, which was painful (*pause*). I left Mevagissey. I returned once but he had gone – his friends said he had gone to sea. He was a bosun various times until he got into trouble and then he'd go back to the decks.

Bloxham: How did he get into trouble?

Sankey: He liked ale too – and grog.

Bloxham: What do you call grog?

Sankey: Rum – he liked rum – he used to go to the various houses of pleasure in the ports and if the women didn't satisfy him he'd throw them out of the window – his friends said they didn't come to any harm because of the rubbish in the streets.

The use of the word 'grog' would seem to be an error, if Sankey's story is to be set in the seventeenth century, when rum was called 'rum' or 'rum-bullion'. 'Grog' is a word from the eighteenth century, supposedly derived from a nickname for the British Admiral Vernon, who in 1740 gave the first order for a sailor's daily ration of rum and water. Vernon was

known as 'Old Grog' because he wore a sea cloak of a coarse
silk and mohair material called 'grogram'.

It has been suggested to me that 'grog' for rum is simply a
word slipped into the regression because the hypnotised man
is using his twentieth-century vocabulary – that the term is
not a major error, even though Sankey makes it quite plain
that he believes firmly he is in the seventeenth century and
his king is Charles II, who reigned for twenty-five years from
1660. Grog or no grog, the regression is moved forward in time
and Sankey has some startling news for Bloxham!

Bloxham: How old are you?
Sankey: In my fiftieth year – getting a bit old – stiff.
Bloxham: Are you still one of the king's men?
Sankey: I've settled down on the coast now – as a magistrate
    – must have been something to do with the troubles.
    They must have thought me worth a lot more than I
    thought myself – I was knighted.
Bloxham: Oh, so you are Sir Arthur now. That's a great
    tribute isn't it?
Sankey: I often wonder.
Bloxham: Which king knighted you?
Sankey: Charles – Charles II.
Bloxham: Tell me about it?
Sankey: There were a number of us who enabled his men –
    one way and another – to gain control over a very dis-
    satisfied people. There were six of us knighted very
    quickly – very brusquely.
Bloxham: What did he say to you?
Sankey: Oh he said he had heard with great appreciation of
    my services to the crown. If there were more men like
    me – God forbid that – if there were more men like me
    his reign would be happier (*pause*) I don't think he could
    have realised what I was until then – the fewer of my
    kind the better!

Sankey's sense of his personal unworthiness seems so real

that he might be quite pleased to learn that no record of his knighthood survives at the Royal College of Arms! This in itself is not especially surprising, for as William Bull explains in his book on knightage – 'In the seventeenth century, a register of knighthood was instituted by King James I. This register is preserved at the College of Arms and extends down to the year 1902, but it is not, and does not claim to be, a complete record of all the knights dubbed in this period.'

As Le Neve makes clear, in his *Pedigrees of the Knights*, the literally golden rule was that if a knight paid to have a coat of arms and to have his arms registered, then he was recorded – otherwise, like so many, he was not. Sankey, the soured old bachelor, was presumably one of these.

The only Sankey recorded as a knight in the seventeenth century was Hierome Sankey, who was knighted in 1658 in Dublin Castle by Henry Cromwell, son of Oliver Cromwell, and this is clearly not our man. The thumbnail description Sankey gave of the reasons for his knighthood could fit almost any time in the rather uneasy reign of Charles II. From the restoration of the monarchy itself in 1660, through the threatened Catholic insurrection of 1678 to the Rye House plot to assassinate the king in 1683, Charles's reign was full of unrest – bogus informers flourished and were well rewarded. Numerous men who seemed to have served the king were knighted.

For Sankey, if he really was knighted, his elevation might have helped overcome a fairly deep rooted sense of inferiority, which he revealed in an exchange with Bloxham early in the regression.

Bloxham: Does the innkeeper know who you are?
Sankey: I think he must do – he's civil – perhaps it's because I carry a cutlass and for no other reason. I am obviously not a gentleman born, therefore I stand or fall by my own efforts – these days one has to fight for one's rights in a public place because the gentry seem to take so much for granted. They have money which we haven't. Every-

one rushes to do their bidding, particularly in the inns – the poorer man is set aside for these gentlemen.

But status in society does not seem to bring happiness to Arthur Sankey. Talking to Bloxham in the last section of the regression, he seems a lonely figure but, much more remarkably, he appears to be drunk! His speech is slurred and the hypnotist can get so little good sense out of him that, without ever seeming to realise the possible cause, he ends the regression with Sankey still droning away, sounding for all the world like a tipsy old man at a warm fireside after a large dinner and too much wine.

If Sankey intends to convey he has been drinking, it is never explicit. It was at the third hearing of this tape that I recognised something was odd and realised what was happening. Young Sankey's drinking habits had caught up with him. Lying on Bloxham's couch, he was getting drunk in a 'previous life'!

Sankey: I must be getting very old – damned if I can remember where I live – is a spot I picked out in my travels in Devon and Cornwall – on the border overlooking the channel where I caught so many of those poor silly people.

Bloxham: Did you get married?

Sankey: No.

Bloxham: Why not? Weren't you lonely?

Sankey: Yes – I was also morose.

Bloxham: And you preferred your ale-pot did you?

Sankey: Yes – an ale-pot doesn't nag!

Bloxham: Have you seen anything of recent fighting between Roundheads and Cavaliers?

Sankey: Roundheads! I've heard that term given to a sect that's rising at the moment – very religious and irreligious – one of man's little jokes I think. The church has cast them out and most of the people require the priest to speak for them to their God. These funny little people jump up and down and say 'we don't need a priest, we

F

can talk to God ourselves' – and they do so in the most alarming fashion.

Bloxham: Are you a religious man yourself?

Sankey: No.

Bloxham: What is your religion?

Sankey: I have no religion – religion is a fairy tale – it is a fairy tale to quiet the nerves of poor little children who require to be led hither and thither. It keeps out the dark and the cold in the winter.

Bloxham: What is the name of the place where you are living?

Sankey: The house is the Elms – it is between two villages – Dog – Dogger's Cross – funny name for a village!

Bloxham: Do you wear a periwig?

Sankey: Dreadful nuisance having to powder it – always put too much on – stuff gets all over my jacket – I have to take it off and brush it.

Bloxham: What clothes do you wear?

Sankey: Blue jacket like the sea – white leggings – black buckled shoes – soft shoes – comfortable.

Arthur Sankey, one of the most human and colourful characters in the Bloxham collection, goes tipsily on – he relates vaguely how local tradesmen give him an interest in their businesses in return for the use of his 'name', and presumably his services as a corruptible magistrate. At last, after two hours, Bloxham has had enough and ends the regression.

Attractive though he is, Sankey for me raises too many factual queries in his story to be rated alongside the best of the Jane Evans regressions and the dramatic story of the gunner's mate in the *Aggie*.

Chapter 13

THE MYSTERY OF HYPNOTISM

M Y historical researches had come to an end, and strangely the tapes seemed to have been corroborated. I was left not with a mystery resolved, but a mystery confirmed. So I decided to turn to the psychologists for their insights into the nature of hypnosis and regression. Librarians sent me books on psychology, on hypnotism and memory. I talked to psychologists and eventually asked a psychiatrist friend, Dr Dafydd Huws, to read a draft of this chapter, to see if perhaps I was talking rubbish.

His verdict surprised me: I had expressed too tentatively my own conclusion that hypnotism had always been misunderstood and that modern psychology knew nothing that could positively disprove Bloxham's theories.

'You could say,' he told me, 'that the mind is an unknown land which we are exploring and that so far we have hardly set one foot outside the boat. Our subject is the mind and yet we can define it only by describing what it does or by discussing the mechanism of the brain – which is like discussing a scene from a film in terms of the projector.'

A poet, he said, might know as much as a psychiatrist about the inner secrets of the human mind. As for this phenomenon of Bloxham's, hypnotised people who appeared to regress to some past life, most practitioners would have absolutely no experience of it. In everyday psychology, regression under hypnosis means the reliving of some scene from an earlier stage of a present life. Regression, back in time beyond the moment of birth, is generally unknown territory, and although individual psychiatrists might find Bloxham's theories unacceptable and be able to postulate their own alternatives, they have no access to any fund of private and professional knowledge by which Bloxham can be proved to be wrong.

The story of hypnotism is itself a saga of two hundred years of misunderstanding, during which medical and other 'expert' opinion has almost invariably jumped to the wrong conclusions.

In the late eighteenth century, the pioneer of hypnotism was the Austrian Friedrich Anton Mesmer, whose colourful experiments with 'Mesmerism', part of his theory of animal magnetism, had captured the public's imagination.

But in Paris, Mesmer's demonstrations and theories were investigated by a committee of scientific 'experts', who denounced Mesmerism as a hoax and Mesmer as an impostor. Mesmer quietly retired from the public eye.

For years, medical journals refused to publish reports of experiments with hypnotism. In 1842, a surgeon who had performed many operations, using hypnosis instead of an anaesthetic, read a paper to the Royal Medical and Chirurgical Society demonstrating the amputation of a leg whilst the patient was hypnotised. The Society agreed afterwards that all record of the experiment should be struck from the minutes, and one prominent member said they had clearly been hoaxed – the person whose leg was amputated had obviously pretended to feel no pain!

But gradually, in the face of much opposition, Mesmerism came to be accepted as a genuine phenomenon, although its name was changed to hypnotism, possibly to diminish the memory of past blunders.

The word 'hypnotism' comes from the Greek 'hypnos' meaning sleep, and accepted definitions of hypnosis, such as Pavlov's, said that it was a form of sleep. But this was another mistake.

The idea that hypnosis was a sort of sleep or state of semi-consciousness was exploded quite recently in a clinical experiment using an electro-encephalograph, a machine which measures the electrical activity of the brain by electrodes attached to the skull.

The first time a hypnotised person was plugged into an EEG it was fully anticipated that the recorded brainwaves would reproduce the pattern for sleep. Instead a hypnotised person invariably has the EEG reading of someone who is fully conscious or wide awake. This discovery caused the old definition of hypnosis as a form of sleep to be abandoned, and the condition is now often referred to somewhat cautiously as 'an altered state of consciousness' – just as perhaps a complex vehicle such as an aeroplane could be referred to as 'an altered piece of metal'.

Although Bloxham's hypnotised subjects can clearly no longer be said to be sleeping, some psychiatrists have discussed the regressions with me as if they were analysing dreams – which is not really foolish since the same theories that apply to fantasies called dreams might equally well apply to fantasies under hypnosis.

Dream and regression are said to be based upon some previous experience. With a dream, a Freudian would say its shape is determined by some half-remembered event of the past day or so, possibly a scene from a book we read. For a Bloxham-style regression, the time scale is said to be longer and the source of the fantasy perhaps a historical novel read some years ago. The significance of either is that from its content, a trained mind would be able to deduce much about our secret thoughts and desires. By our fantasies do they claim to know us.

Of course a dream is a much more familiar phenomenon than a Bloxham-style regression, but it is surprising how the great men of psychology have disagreed over the cause and meaning of dreams. In 1900, Freud in his *Interpretation of Dreams* said that the meaning of a dream was that it expressed the fulfilment of a wish, in dramatised and disguised form. Symbolism was the key to comprehension: for instance a snake represented a penis and a box or basket a vagina.

Erikson in 1954 played down symbolism and said the actual content of the dream should be taken more seriously – in other words, if you went to him you could confess to dreaming of a snake charmer at work without being put on tranquillisers! French and Fromm then suggested in 1963 that a dream was an attempt to solve a problem. While in 1944, Carl Jung had suggested that certain figures that tend to recur in dreams personified universal notions such as God, mother, wise old man, good and evil, or aspects of sexuality. He also warned his colleagues 'not to have any preconceived, doctrinaire opinions about the statements made by dreams.'

Psychologists have other interpretations too which allegedly can be applied to our fantasies. But it appeared obvious that a closer parallel than a dream to a Bloxham regression was the relatively common phenomenon of an ordinary regression under hypnosis.

It is difficult for a layman to grasp that, as an ordinary feature of hypnosis, an adult can relive the days of his childhood, recalling long forgotten events, and becoming to all intents and purposes a young child once again. About this form of regression it is never suggested the hypnotised person is fantasising, weaving some tissue of lies about some long forgotten event, or something he had read in a newspaper last year.

Yet, as far as I can tell, there is only one difference in practice between an ordinary regression to childhood and Bloxham's version: one hypnotist asks his subject to go back to the age of seven, and the other asks him to go back to a time before he was born. Is it not possible that both these essentially similar techniques produce similar results – the hypnotised person expresses a genuine and personal experience of the past to which he has been directed?

It is normally held that hypnotised people are incapable of volunteering a lie, so why should they not be believed when, in a trance, they say that they are living some centuries ago?

Well, one definition of hypnotism is that the person in the trance has surrendered his will or ego to the hypnotist, and anyone who has seen a stage hypnotist at work will know that the person in the trance will accept whatever reality the hypnotist cares to implant in his mind. The subject lies inert, a neutral personality incapable of volunteering a lie or creating a fantasy without some command from the hypnotist. But when it comes, he will, if told, bark like a dog or accept that he is an iron bridge and support the weight of half a dozen men.

The nub of the rational argument, for those who say the Bloxham Tapes have to be fantasies because the implications of their being real are unthinkable, is that although Bloxham never tells his subjects to regress to any particular time or personality, he must be controlling them in some way; and he does command them to go back to the past, to a time before they were born. Is this enough to trigger off a fantasy? Can that simple instruction cause them to fabricate an entire life in the same way that the command to be a dog would cause them to bark and howl?

The person regressed does not respond to Bloxham's instruction with one simple lie, but presents instantly a tightly knit fabric of fantasy which can be attested historically. Bloxham certainly does not prompt them with facts or feed them ideas, I have myself witnessed that his questioning is deliberately neutral. And his subjects are not stooges for I have seen him regress comparative strangers. The historical 'lives' are somehow waiting in the mind of the person in the trance, ready for the hypnotist to bring them out, for such detailed and deeply felt 'lives' could not possibly be spur-of-the-moment fantasies.

The psychiatrist, Dr Anthony Storr, gave me an explanation. He listened patiently to two of the Bloxham Tapes and told me he had no doubts whatever about the integrity of Bloxham or the people he had hypnotised. He said candidly that reincarnation was not an explanation he could consider seriously, and his firm conclusion was that Bloxham's regressions were examples of cryptomnesia, that is fantasies based upon some long forgotten historical novel or magazine article.

Dr Storr gave me a quotation to chew on: 'Most of us have a B movie running in our heads most of the time.'

A valid observation, since we all fantasise and sometimes

become imaginatively involved with stories we read or items we see on television. But would it explain why Jane Evans should have *six* B movies running in her head at the same time, and why this intelligent young woman, who has a good memory, cannot recall the source material for any one of six historically attestable 'fantasies'? The obscurity of some aspects of her historical knowledge is also puzzling.

One of the best known recorded examples of cryptomnesia makes an interesting comparison with the Bloxham Tapes. A woman under hypnosis vividly described scenes from the reign of King Richard II of England. But she felt no unbidden compulsion actually to assume the identity of any of the characters she was talking about, and, from her detached account, observers thought at first that some ghost or spirit guide was somehow enabling her to see into the past. Eventually, still under hypnosis, she revealed she was describing scenes from the historical novel *Countess Maud* which she had read as a child of twelve.

If Bloxham's subjects feel obliged to describe some scene, whose origin is perhaps a historical novel, why do they also not simply see and describe it as they would a play enacted for their benefit, without becoming an on-stage actor? Alternatively, since hypnotised people usually respond truthfully to questions, why do they not reply to Bloxham's first question 'What can you see?' by saying 'I can see nothing – all is dark,' as they frequently say in other parts of the regressions?

The extent to which people under hypnosis will indulge in personal fantasies, without specific prompting by the hypnotist, is open to question. There is no doubt, however, that under hypnosis the memory is greatly stimulated and it would be quite possible to resurrect the outline of some forgotten book or short story. A hypnotised builder once described a wall he had built thirty years earlier. He told researchers its size, shape, location and the exact number of bricks he had used. The wall was later inspected and it was as he claimed – down to the last brick.

In this instance, the builder, regressed into the past by thirty years, had thus revealed nothing that was not the literal truth. There was no exaggeration or fantasising, no grafting fiction on to the facts, it was simply that regression under hypnosis enabled a man to precisely recall past events no longer available to the normally conscious mind.

Another dramatic feature of the trance is the hypnotised person's total belief in the reality of the events unfolding in the mind. Lying on a couch in Bloxham's consulting room, Jane Evans actually 'lives out' her strange experiences. Whether founded in fantasy or fact, her personal sense of reality has been given an added dimension – she can smell flowers invisible to the onlooker, can see and touch objects visible only in her mind and can feel pain, physical and emotional, inspired by those secret events.

In hypnotism, this altered sense of reality is well known. A brain surgeon, telling me that hypnotism was insufficiently used and understood by his profession, quoted an experiment – a man in a trance was told, seemingly more in the name of science than humanity, that a quite ordinary coin placed in the small of his back was red hot. He not only felt pain but his skin reproduced a mark like a burn.

Presumably this is why Bloxham, with his long experience as a hypnotist, was always quick to wake people up at the first signs of real suffering. Two of Jane Evans's regressions he ended smartly when she began to speak of and show signs of fever, though he had more difficulty in ending the trance of Graham Huxtable when his leg had apparently been shot away and he was screaming in uncontrollable pain. Also the hypnotist promptly ended the regression of my colleague when she went into her imaginary but very 'real' labour.

Hypnotism is thus clearly a doorway to the secret world of a strange and powerfully altered state of consciousness, but an aspect we too often take for granted is the incredible ability of the hypnotist to shut that door behind us, so that even the physical reality of our own bodies loses significance – no drug has been given to make us unconscious, we are apparently wide awake, yet under hypnosis our teeth can be pulled, our limbs sawn off and women may painlessly give birth to children.

Reality it would seem begins and ends in the mind, whose secrets and complexities we are far from understanding. The practice of hypnotherapy, curing by suggestion under hypnosis, further bears this out. During repeated sessions, the patient is told by his hypnotherapist that black is white – that his asthma has vanished, his warts have gone away, he has stopped stammering and has no desire to smoke. The mind believes and the body will adjust accordingly.

Even outside hypnotism, this ability of the mind to control the physical is demonstrable. An international film star recently became reunited with his stepfather on being assured by surgeons that the old man was dying from incurable cancer. It was an emotional reunion and the old man was very moved. Yet from the day the pair settled their differences, he began to recover, as if his physical health were being regulated by his new desire to live.

But to demonstrate that events in the mind of the hypnotised person can appear to be totally real does not prove that they are real in an historical sense. Bloxham's subjects experience their 'past lives' to the full and believe them to be real, but as Jung said: 'A belief proves to me only the phenomenon of belief, not the content of the belief.'

Of course, the corroboration of history is real and admissible evidence, and so are indications of personality changes within the regressions, which suggest that it is not the everyday Jane Evans who is just below the skin of every character from the past she believes herself to be.

Jane Evans, the South Wales housewife, is a settled married woman, but her regressions display widely varying attitudes towards sex and morality. In one regression she is a carefree seventeen-year-old girl who has had several lovers, in another she is a shy and rather solemn teenager with no interest in men; on two occasions she is married happily, once with children and once without, and, in the most extreme case, she is a nun in a convent with faint regrets that she never married.

Similarly there are remarkable changes in other regressions, such as that in Graham Huxtable when he becomes the gunner's mate. Comparing the present-day Huxtable to the earthy sailor, neither Graham nor I can find any point of contact or similarity. In experience and attitudes, the sailor is a quite different sort of man – nor can I conceive that a grim regression of that sort can be explained as a 'fulfilment of a wish' or 'an effort at solving a problem'. Such explanations are mildly ridiculous.

On the other hand, for all the reality of Bloxham's regressions, there is one apparent oddity. Bloxham's subjects do not speak in the natural languages of the people they imagine themselves to be. Jane Evans as the Roman wife Livonia does not for instance speak in Latin.

In some cases of regression this phenomenon of speaking in tongues is said actually to have occurred. Professor Stevenson of the University of Virginia tells of a hypnotised American who spoke an eighteenth-century Swedish dialect, although previously he had shown no ability to speak Swedish in any form.

The closest Bloxham has come to this is that he tells me he once hypnotised a man who spoke a language the hypnotist took to be German. But since Bloxham could not understand a word his subject was saying, he abandoned the session and never renewed it.

But people vary in their responses to hypnotism and perhaps only a few exceptions can regress with such an intensity of recollection. It is clear too that different aspects of memory are stored in different parts of the brain and no one is quite certain what areas are being activated under hypnosis.

Memories, in any case, are frequently divorced from speech. A recollection of a piece of music can be auditory only, a painting can be a purely visual memory: recall an incident from your early childhood and you will not express it with the limited vocabulary and speech patterns of a five-year-old, you will translate the incident into your present language.

One of Bloxham's subjects told me being regressed was a mainly visual experience supplemented by 'words which just pop into your head'.

Another said: 'It was seeing strange pictures for the first time, feeling completely new thoughts and sensations and having some difficulty in finding words to describe it all when answering Bloxham's questions.'

Perhaps the closest anyone came, in the Bloxham regressions I have heard, to using a strange tongue was Huxtable as the gunner's mate. Some of his naval slang and archaic phrases he could not understand himself, when he came out of his trance, and they made no sense to me – in fact some were wrongly transcribed, until naval historians at Greenwich heard the tape and explained their meaning.

Even the latest theories on memory seem to provide more questions than answers. Long- and short-term memories are held to be different processes, they involve separate storage areas in the brain and some memories may be chemically activated and others electrically.

But it is accepted that hypnosis and electrical stimulation of the brain can unlock memories stored in the deep recesses of the mind, which are complex and minutely detailed to an extent the man in the street would find incredible.

Quite recently a patient under anaesthetic had part of his brain stimulated by an electrode, which suddenly caused him to relive, in a series of flashbacks, events from his past. Scenes came to him far more vividly than normal memories 'as if the electrode had started a film strip on which were registered the details of a past even the patient had long since forgotten. As long as the electrode is held in place, the experience of the former life goes on. When the electrode is removed, the experience stops abruptly.'

The Bloxham hypothesis is that something similar to that process occurs just as spontaneously when hypnosis, that other recognised stimulant of the memory, is applied. The difference is that the new flashback is not to memories of our childhood, but, as the subjects themselves indicate, to scenes from beyond birth – vestiges of a forgotten previous existence, stored in a remote area of our largely uncharted minds.

For those who believe that such a notion is too fanciful and irrational, that great thinker Dr Carl Jung should perhaps be given the last word, from *Memories, Dreams, Reflections:*

> . . . nowadays most people identify themselves almost exclusively with their consciousness and imagine they are only what they know about themselves. Yet anyone with even a smattering of psychology can see how limited this knowledge is.
>
> Rationalism and doctrinaireism are the diseases of our time; they pretend to have all the answers. But a great deal will yet be discovered which our present limited view would have ruled out as impossible. Our concepts of space and time have only approximate validity, and there is therefore a wide field for minor and major deviations. In view of all this, I lend an attentive ear to the strange myths of the psyche, and take a careful look at the varied events that come my way, regardless of whether or not they fit in with my theoretical postulates.

Chapter 14

BETWEEN MY HAT AND MY BOOTS –
THE ANCIENT BELIEF IN REINCARNATION

WHAT other evidence then, I had to ask myself, is there in man's experience to support the idea of previous existence, that we all do in fact have more lives than one?

A belief in reincarnation can be traced back for six centuries before the birth of Christ. This creed, which the Greeks called metempsychosis, has been accepted at some time by most of the world's races and religions – the ancient Egyptians and Greeks, Hindus and Buddhists, Muslims and early Christians, the Red Indians of North America and the Celts of my native Wales. Outstanding individuals in every age have believed they lived before, from Plato to Napoleon and from Plutarch to Henry Ford.

But someone rather less eminent, a television dramatist, aroused my curiosity about the extent of this belief. Over a drink in a bar, he told me of a horoscope that was once prepared for him. At the foot was written – 'in a previous life you were a crippled musician.'

The sentence shocked him, because since childhood he had been haunted by a secret and persistent dream that he was crippled. The nightmare was so powerful that as a youth he had begun to walk with a limp. He thought of consulting a psychiatrist, but gradually the dream faded.

Today, he wonders if the astrologist was right and he really was, in some previous life, a lame musician. He set me wondering what evidence there might be in the world for a belief in reincarnation. What is the background against which we can judge the Bloxham Tapes?

Dr Stevenson of the University of Virginia, whom I have already quoted, has said that many children, in both East and West, have memories of a previous life, but as they grow older these fade. Parents rarely encourage their children to carry on with strange talk about a life in another time.

Recently, Dr Stevenson has investigated the case of an Englishman, Edward Ryall, who says he has full recollection of a life as John Fletcher, a west-of-England farmer killed at the battle of Sedgemoor in 1685. Ryall says his memories began as a child, but were suppressed by his father who feared the boy might be labelled an idiot.

Stevenson has studied numerous eastern cases of such memories. One of the most famous is that of Shanti Deva, born in Delhi in 1926, who at the age of seven announced that in a previous life she had been a married woman in the town of Muttra and had died giving birth to a third child. Her name then had been Ludgi.

At the age of nine, Shanti Deva recognised a man she said had been her cousin, and later she met a second man she said was her former husband.

This man admitted that his wife, named Ludgi, had died in childbirth ten years earlier. Shanti Deva was taken to Muttra and is said to have recognised the two oldest children of the family but not the third – that is the one during whose birth she herself, as she claimed, had died.

Both Stevenson, and Colin Wilson in *The Occult*, have recorded numerous cases like this. And knowledge of pre-existence is not limited to children or the East. Pythagoras had full recall of a life as Euphorbus, who was killed at the siege of Troy. Napoleon several times insisted he was a reincarnation of Charlemagne, and Salvador Dali has said he was once the Spanish mystic St John of the Cross: '. . . I can remember vividly my life as St John, of experiencing divine union, of understanding the dark night of the soul of which he writes with so much feeling. I can remember the monastery and I can remember many of St John's fellow monks.'

Bringing the argument down to the level of the rest of us, there is a relatively common experience which believers in rebirth would argue is evidence of reincarnation. The Yogi Ramacharaka in his book *Gnani Yoga* asks:

Who has not experienced the consciousness of having felt the thing before – having thought it some time in the dim past? Who has not witnessed new scenes that appear old, very old? Who has not met persons for the first time, whose presence awakened memories of a past, lying far back in the misty ages of long ago? Who has not been seized at times with the consciousness of a mighty 'oldness' of soul? Who has not heard music, often entirely new compositions, which somehow awakens memories of similar strains, scenes, places, faces, voices, lands, associations and events, sounding dimly on the strings of memory as the breezes of harmony float over them? Who has not gazed at some old painting or piece of statuary, with the sense of having seen it all before? Who has not lived through events which brought with them a certainty of being merely a repetition of some shadowy occurrences away back in lives lived long ago?

Charles Dickens had such an experience. Walking one evening in the Italian town of Ferrara, he looked at a bridge near a hollow and felt suddenly – 'If I had been murdered there in some former life, I could not have seemed to remember the place more thoroughly or with a more emphatic chilling of the blood.'

Sir Walter Scott wrote in his diary of something similar:

Yesterday at dinner-time, I was strangely haunted by what I would call the sense of pre-existence, a confused idea that nothing that passed was said for the first time; that the same topics had been discussed and the same persons had stated the same opinions on them. The sensation was so strong as to resemble what is called the mirage in the desert.

Another writer, Louis Bromfield, believed his obsession with France was caused by some 'earlier knowledge'. Eventually, he went to live there: 'Nothing ever surprised or astonished me; no landscape, no forest, no chateau, no Paris street, no provincial town ever seemed strange. I had seen it all before. It was always a country and its people a people whom I knew well and intimately.'

Joan Grant, who writes historical novels, goes one better.

During the last twenty years, seven books of mine have been published as historical novels, which to me are biographies of previous lives I have known. . . . From early childhood, often to my extreme discomfort, I was sometimes aware beyond the usual range of the five senses. I tried to ignore the implications of this awareness, but it was too insistent; so in an attempt to understand what was happening, I laboriously trained the faculty of far memory.

A whole host of modern Western writers have also written of their belief in rebirth. The Irish poet W. B. Yeats, Sir Arthur Conan Doyle, Goethe, Maeterlinck, Victor Hugo, Balzac, Flaubert, Tolstoy, Louisa May Alcott, Edgar Allan Poe and many more have been quoted in *Reincarnation, An East-West Anthology*, edited by Joseph Head and S. L. Cranston.

Many philosophers and psychologists from William James onwards have taken seriously belief in reincarnation, as have industrialists, including Henry Ford, and scientists such as the British physicist Sir Oliver Lodge and the American inventor Thomas Edison.

Of course, when a scientist agrees with a theologian it does not necessarily mean they are making good sense. In the seventeenth century, the British scientist Sir Isaac Newton and the Irish Archbishop James Usher shared the opinion that the world was created in the year 4004 BC! But neither, as far as I know, ever asserted any faith in reincarnation!

A firm believer was the American Benjamin Franklin, printer, writer, statesman in the American War of Independence, pioneer of electricity, inventor of bi-focal spectacles and a new kind of stove. Franklin was once described as 'the first civilised American'. From the age of sixteen he accepted that he had lived before.

He was among the first to comprehend the Law of the Conservation of Matter. For him the idea that matter changed its form but could never be entirely 'lost' was a simple extension of his belief that on dying we were reborn.

> I say that when I see nothing annihilated, and not even a drop of water wasted, I cannot expect the annihilation of souls, or believe that He will suffer the daily waste of millions of minds ready made that now exist, and put Himself to the continual trouble of making new ones. Thus, finding myself to exist in the world, I believe I shall, in some shape or other, always exist.

When he died in 1790, aged 84, Franklin left one of the most famous of all epitaphs, written many years earlier to express his belief in reincarnation:

The Body
of
Benjamin Franklin
Printer
Like the Cover of an Old Book
Its Contents Torn Out
And Stripped of its Lettering and Gilding
Lies Here, Food for Worms.
But the Work Shall Not Be Lost
For It Will (As He Believed) Appear Once More
In a New and More Elegant Edition
Revised and Corrected
By
The Author

A modern scientist to endorse Franklin's analogy between reincarnation and the laws of physics was the American astrophysicist, Dr Heber D. Curtis, who wrote:

> I personally find it impossible to regard Handel's 'Largo', Keats's 'Ode to a Grecian Urn', and the higher ethics as mere by-products of the chemical interaction of a collection of hydrocarbon molecules. With energy, matter, space and time continuous, with nothing lost or wasted, are we ourselves the only manifestation that comes to an end, ceases, is annihilated at three score years and ten?

In the last century, a courageous Unitarian Minister, the Reverend William R. Alger, devoted half his life to a study of reincarnation. The conclusion of the first edition in 1860 of his *A Critical History of the Doctrine of Future Life* was that the idea was a plausible delusion and unworthy of belief. But after a further fifteen years of research, he published a second edition and announced that he was a convert to reincarnation!

The reasons why a modern Christian too might find the notion plausible, were best put by an English minister, the Reverend Leslie D. Weatherhead, in 1957:

> The intelligent Christian asks not only that life should be just, but that it shall make sense. Does the idea of reincarnation help here? I think it does. Let us suppose that a very depraved or entirely materialistic person dies. Let us suppose that from a religious point of view he has entirely misused his earth life. Will his translation to a spiritual plane do all that needs doing? Will it not be like putting a person who has never given himself any chance to understand music, into an everlasting concert. . .? Can a man who has entirely neglected spiritual things be happy in a spiritual environment? If you say 'oh well, he can learn in the next phase' — can he? Doesn't such a speculation make the earth life meaningless? I don't think we shall be able to skip the examinations of life like that. It would be as incongruous

and unsound as telling a medical student, who failed his qualifying examination, not to bother, but go on treating people as if he had qualified. If I fail to pass those examinations in life which can only be taken while I dwell in a physical body, shall I not have to come back and take them again?

In modern times in the west, the most fervent propaganda for the idea of reincarnation has come from the Theosophical Society, founded in 1875 by that remarkable Russian mystic Helena Petrovna Blavatsky. The influence of the society and its many published works has been world-wide, and the teachings and doctrines of the east have been placed on the bookshelves of the west.

Of reincarnation, Blavatsky wrote: 'It is only this doctrine, we say, that can explain to us the mysterious problem of Good and Evil, and reconcile man to the terrible and apparent injustice of life . . . there is not an accident in our lives, not a misshapen day, or a misfortune, that could not be traced back to our own doings in this or another life.'

In theosophy, like the religions of the east, the Law of Karma goes hand in hand with reincarnation. This spiritual law of cause and effect says that our thoughts and behaviour in one life determine how and when we will be reborn in the next. The aim, in eastern religions, is eventually to escape the rebirth cycle by attaining 'Nirvana' or 'Moksha', a state of perfect wisdom.

The *Bardo Thodol*, or *Tibetan Book of the Dead*, is a strange list of events in the mind of a dead man from the moment of death until rebirth. In his foreword to the German translation, Jung defined Karma as 'a sort of psychic theory of heredity based on the hypothesis of reincarnation'.

Jung added – 'psychic heredity does exist. That is to say there is inheritance of psychic characteristics such as predisposition to disease, traits of character, special gifts and so forth.'

By extending Jung's assertion, the child prodigy may be seen as someone who has retained knowledge or ability from a previous life. Mozart from the age of four was able to play difficult pieces on the piano and to compose works superior to those of many mature composers. There are numerous more modern examples – musicians such as Yehudi Menuhin, chess players such as Bobby Fischer and Jose Capablanca – who displayed extraordinary virtuosity when children. The theory is not restricted to geniuses – an example could be any child with a strongly developed personality or some special aptitude or ability not explicable by his heredity or environment.

The actual process of reincarnation, described in detail in the ancient *Tibetan Book of the Dead*, so conforms to the principles of modern psychology that Dr Jung wrote: 'Every serious minded reader must ask himself whether these wise old monks might not after all have caught a glimpse of the fourth dimension and twitched the veil from the greatest of life's secrets.'

In the west, the teaching was powerfully expressed by the ancient Greek philosophers Plato, Pythagoras, Aristotle, Plotinus and Plutarch. As Plutarch wrote: 'Every soul is ordained to wander between incarnations in the region between the moon and the earth for a term. . . .'

In ancient Israel too, cradle of Christianity, the belief was strong. The Jewish historian Josephus says plainly that, of the three main sects of Israel, the Essenes and the Pharisees both taught reincarnation and only the Sadducees did not. Rebirth was also one of the Inner Doctrines of the Kabbalah of the Hebrews.

There are numerous references in both the Old and New Testaments of the Bible. Moses is believed to be a reincarnation of Adam's son Abel, and Adam himself was expected to be reborn as the Messiah. The closing words of the Old Testament predict the rebirth of the prophet Elijah, and the Book of Matthew mentions Elias reborn as John the Baptist. And when Christ asked his disciples – 'who do men say that I am?' – he is told, either John the Baptist, Elias or Jeremias.

For over five hundred years after Christ, reincarnation was a belief freely held by many Christians. It was taught by powerful sects such as the Gnostics and the Manichaeans, and was declared a heresy, in very doubtful circumstances, only by the Fifth Ecumenical Council of AD 553, seemingly without the approval of the Pope!

The conflict was caused by the earlier writings and teachings of Origen, one of the most influential Christian theologians of all time, who was born in Alexandria in AD 185. Origen, revered by men such as St Jerome and St Gregory, strongly urged the philosophy of reincarnation taught by the Ancient Greeks:

> Every soul comes into this world strengthened by the victories or weakened by the defeats of its previous life. Its place in this world as a vessel appointed to honour or dishonour is determined by its previous merits or demerits. Its work in this world determines its place in the world which is to follow this. . . .

But the Emperor Justinian in the sixth century decided for himself that Origen's teaching of reincarnation was a heresy. He convened the Fifth Ecumenical Council and there was never much doubt about the outcome. Justinian invited one hundred and fifty-nine bishops from the east and only six from the west, where Origen's teachings were more widely accepted. Pope Vergilius protested that there should be equal representation of east and west, and refused to attend the council, although he was in Constantinople where the session was held.

Today, Catholic scholars debate the legality of the Fifth Council and the fifteen Articles of Anathema, which it appears the Pope never sanctioned. But the persecution and the burning of 'heretics' across Europe began in the sixth century with the publication of the first article:

'If anyone assert the pre-existence of souls, and shall assert the monstrous restoration which follows from it, let him be anathema (cursed).'

That was the parting of the ways for Christianity and reincarnation. For centuries, Christian Europe was ablaze with holy bonfires in France, Spain, Bulgaria and elsewhere. Some persecuted sects turned for sanctuary to the Arab world. In the sixth century, the Prophet Mohammed learned of reincarnation as taught by the ancient Greeks from the monks of a Nestorian monastery at Busra. The Muslim holy book, the *Koran*, written in Mohammed's time, says explicitly:

'God generates beings and sends them back over and over again until they return to Him.'

In the west, that Fifth Ecumenical Council which rejected the teachings of Plato and Aristotle proved a key event in hastening the onset of the Dark Ages, the centuries when the light of Classical learning was virtually extinguished in Europe. In the Arab world too, the doctrine of reincarnation was never fully accepted, and the belief was sustained over the centuries only by the influence of the Sufis, a Persian sect of mystics.

The oldest and most consistent exponents of the creed have been the Hindus of India, with their ancient sacred texts the *Vedas* and the *Brahmanas*. Sir Matthew Arnold caught the essence of their ageless message in his translation of the *Bhagavad Gita*:

Never the spirit was born; the spirit shall cease to be
    never;
Never was time it was not. End and beginning are dreams!
Birthless and deathless and changeless remaineth the spirit
    forever.
Death hath not touched it at all, dead though the house of
    it seems.

And although for most of us in the west today, religion, any religion, is seen as just another bromide, the pat definitions of science on the finite nature of man are no more convincing. Most of us suspect, deep down, that there is something more to the human species than meets the eye of the average scientist.

The American Walt Whitman, a believer in reincarnation, expressed his faith in just two lines:

> I pass death with the dying, and birth with the new
> washed babe,
> And am not contained between my hat and my boots.

Chapter 15

A LIGHT IN THE DARKNESS

SOME two years after my first visit to Arnall Bloxham, I sat down to reflect again on the meaning of the Bloxham Tapes. Were they really the evidence the old hypnotist believed them to be, for the ancient belief in the reincarnation of souls? And if not, what were they?

It was May 1976, and Bloxham was now in hospital, hopefully not for long, but he was quietly pleased that the book was nearly ready for publication and the film I had made with Magnus Magnusson was about to be edited. Our work was reaching its conclusion.

Two weeks before suddenly being admitted to hospital, Bloxham had asked me when was publication day, and added quietly: 'I have a feeling that by the autumn I won't be here. I don't mind dying, not in the least, but it is possible I won't be here to read the book or see the film.'

Whether Bloxham had sensed the onset of some temporary failure in his health, I had no way of knowing. But I went to his house a few afternoons later and read him a draft of the chapter about himself, and gave him an idea of what the historical researches had revealed. He nodded his head and said 'That's fine, that's fine.'

It was only then that I realised that throughout the months of my regular visits he had never shown any curiosity about the historical researches into the regressions – the thought in fact had never crossed his mind that the history books might do anything but confirm the authenticity of his tapes. Arnall Bloxham's faith in his regressions, like his belief in reincarnation, was absolute.

As for me, what conclusions could I come to? Of one thing

both Magnusson and I were certain – the Bloxham Tapes were genuine, there was no question of fraud or hoax. Unwitting fantasies they just *might* be, but the regressions are undoubtedly 'real'. Every historian and psychologist who has heard them was of the same opinion – and there is always the case of my own nominee, Beata Lipman, hypnotised by Bloxham and instantly regressed at the first time of asking.

It had been impressive too watching Jane Evans being regressed once again for the benefit of the television camera. After an interval of more than five years, this hypnotised woman had reiterated, with only minor differences, the complex outlines of two of the original Bloxham Tapes. Largely unaltered and unembellished, her stories seemed to be products more of memory than imagination. Any 'Walter Mitty'-type fantasy is surely not a static thing? The scripts for the 'B' movies which apparently go on in our heads are surely rewritten almost annually? As we change, our fantasies change with us, or so I would have thought.

Then again, some of the regressions were so consistently and surprisingly accurate historically. Not just places, names and dates were corroborated but so was the 'sense of period', the background detail of dress and attitude. For me a historical fantasy should be nine tenths imagination and one part history – but the Bloxham Tapes were not like that. Nor can I even guess how Jane Evans was familiar with some of the facts and locations she speaks of with such assurance. She has, after all, never set foot in York nor the Loire Valley of France, and she visited America only after she had recorded her regression as the American nun.

Neither Magnus Magnusson nor I had anticipated at the outset that the Bloxham Tapes would be corroborated by the history books to such an extent. I knew it was not uncommon for people down the ages to claim 'memories' of some past incarnation, especially in those parts of the world where rebirth is a generally held belief, and people feel they can talk freely about their past lives without being regarded as peculiar. But hardly ever, it seemed, had researchers actually delved back into history to discover whether these stories could be verified. Our findings in the Bloxham cases appeared to challenge our whole Western notion of the realities of life and death.

Yet in the end, my search for the truth about the Bloxham Tapes had left me with no certainties, indeed with new mysteries.

But the quest itself had been enriching, I realised as I tried to formulate some conclusions. As a concept, reincarnation had become real to me not simply through the Bloxham Tapes but through the writings of men of high intellect who had believed in it down the ages. It was a genuine addition to those rationally unprovable concepts of Western society; God and the notions of life after death.

I had learned also that modern psychology is full of fascinating theories and wise hints about how to lead a mentally healthy life, but has no sure knowledge relating either to reincarnation or the Bloxham Tapes. The totem pole, for any who worship at this shrine and have not glanced up lately, is still in the shape of a huge question mark.

Nevertheless, there is still a query against the tapes themselves: it is just feasible that they are a series of four hundred fantasies. But any automatic acceptance of the rational argument against them is surely prejudged – loaded by the assertion that fantasies are acceptable explanations for certain ideas in the mind of man, and reincarnation and the like are not. The world seems flat and therefore flat it is.

Was Jane Evans's belief that Jacques Coeur had a 'golden apple' just a lucky guess, and the finding of the crypt at York a mere coincidence? Did Graham Huxtable's knowledge of life at sea two hundred years ago come from a book and his own imagination?

Some of the regressions are more impressive than others, and some certainly could be fantasies – the mind and imagination deal in both fiction and fact. But it needs only one regression to be 'real' for many accepted ideas about life to be turned upside down.

My own view is that the rationalists are not entitled to any walk-over. The Bloxham Tapes have been researched and there is no evidence they are fantasies. In our present state of knowledge about them, they appear to convey exactly what they claim: a genuine knowledge and experience of the past.

Rationalists must grit their teeth and bear with me when I remind them that my grandparents would have locked me up in the barn until I was sober if I had prophesied I would work for something called 'television' by which people in Australia could watch 'live' events occurring on the opposite side of the world. My own imagination still reels from the implications of a more modern scientific pronouncement – that matter and energy are the same thing, so that if I could throw my pen hard enough at the wall it would vanish into pure energy!

There is so much in life that is unknown or barely guessed at, that we should not conclude too readily that fantasy or reincarnation are the only alternatives which might explain the Bloxham Tapes. Extra-sensory perception, the acquisition of knowledge beyond the reach of the senses, is believed real by many. Parapsychologists in various parts of the world have claimed some success for their experiments.

It has been suggested that telepathy, one aspect of ESP, might be responsible for the Bloxham Tapes. Could Bloxham be capable of transmitting the historical outlines of the regressions to the hypnotised minds of all those different people?

I think not. His surprise at much of what he is told during the regressions is quite genuine, and at eighty years of age he does not have the historian's grasp to prepare the narratives, nor the showman's skill to be a ventriloquist with a hypnotised dummy. More conclusively, during Jane Evans's regression as Alison I handed Bloxham a paper with questions which occurred to me during the session. He put the questions and we elicited new information, which he could hardly have prepared for in advance. Nor could he telepathically have plucked the answers from my mind, because at that stage I didn't know them!

There are other possible theories. Could there be some abstract pool of collective knowledge or experience to which the hypnotised mind could have access? A sort of clairvoyance under hypnosis?

Could we have race memories locked away in our minds somewhere? After all, our ancestors in a tiny speck of human seed determined the colour of our hair, the rate at which we would blink our eyes, and settled on us aspects of behaviour called 'instinct'. Could some memory of the traumas they faced in their own lives have also been transmitted in that micro-coded specification for the construction of a present day human being?

Then again, what is 'historical reality' in terms of time and space? Dr Jung, in *Memories, Dreams, Reflections* once more, expressed the view that scenes from past times could be seen or experienced by people living in the present by what he called 'synchronicity'. He quotes as an example his own experience one night in 1924 when he was persistently woken up by an awareness of a band of young men playing music and singing outside his home. When he opened the window the night was still. Months later, he discovered that in medieval times groups of local young men, about to leave to fight in the wars, used to meet for a farewell celebration on the site of his house. Somehow his mind had been able to 'plug in' to a 'recording' of that scene.

But none of these explanations fits too well, and there is scant evidence to support their application to the Bloxham Tapes. Bloxham's people are surely either fantasising – or telling the literal truth, that is they are having a genuine personal experience of a past age. I am in addition impressed by the fact that Bloxham's techniques and the phenomena he produces are so close to those involved in ordinary age-regression under hypnosis; and when a hypnotised subject goes back to his childhood and remembers facts seemingly beyond human recall, we accept what he says without question.

So Bloxham's twenty years of work must constitute at least a prima facie case for reincarnation. And if his tapes do no more than compel us to re-examine our beliefs about our nature, and our fate, that in itself will be an achievement given to few. As Jung wrote, near the end of his own life: 'As far as we can discover the sole purpose of human existence is to kindle a light in the darkness of mere being.'

SELECTED BIBLIOGRAPHY

BERNSTEIN, M., *The Search for Bridey Murphy*, Hutchinson, London, 1956

BLOXHAM, DULCIE, *Who was Ann Ockendon?*, Neville Spearman, London, 1958

CLOWES, SIR W. LAIRD, *The Royal Navy*, (7 vols.), Sampson Low & Co., 1897–1903

DOBSON, R. B., *The Jews of mediaeval York and the Massacre of March, 1190*, St. Anthony's Press, York, 1974

EVANS-WENTZ, W. Y., *The Tibetan Book of the Dead*, Oxford University Press, 1927

HEAD, J. and CRANSTON, S. L., (eds.) *Reincarnation: an East-West Anthology*, Theosophical Publishing House, Wheaton, 1968

HEIM, GERARD, *L'Etrange Destin de Jacques Coeur*, Paris

JUNG, C. G., *Memories, Dreams, Reflections*, Collins & Routledge, 1963

KERR, A. B., *Jacques Coeur, Merchant Prince of the Middle Ages*, Scribner, New York, 1927

KOESTLER, ARTHUR, *The Act of Creation*, Hutchinson, 1964

MARCUS, G. J., *A Naval History of England*, Longman's, 1961

MATTINGLY, GARRETT, *Catherine of Aragon*, Jonathan Cape, 1942

NICHOLLS, F. F., *Honest Thieves, the violent heyday of English smuggling*, Heinemann, London, 1973

RAMACHARAKA, YOGI (pseud. William Walker Atkinson), *A Series of Lessons in Gnani Yoga, the Yoga of Wisdom*, L. N. Fowler, London, 1917

RICHMOND, Sir I. A., *Roman Britain*, Jonathan Cape, London, 1963

RYALL, E. W., *Second Time Round*, Neville Spearman, Jersey, 1974

WILSON, COLIN, *The Occult*, Hodder & Stoughton, London, 1971